Infinite Feathers

QUILTING DESIGNS

American Quilter's Society

P. O. Box 3290 • Paducah, KY 42002-3290
www.AQSquilt.com

Anita
Shackelford

Located in Paducah, Kentucky, the American Quilter's Society (AQS) is dedicated to promoting the accomplishments of today's quilters. Through its publications and events, AQS strives to honor today's quiltmakers and their work and to inspire future creativity and innovation in quiltmaking.

EDITORS: SHELLEY HAWKINS AND BONNIE K. BROWNING
TECHNICAL EDITOR: HELEN SQUIRE
GRAPHIC DESIGN: LYNDA SMITH
COVER DESIGN: MICHAEL BUCKINGHAM
PHOTOGRAPHY: CHARLES R. LYNCH (UNLESS OTHERWISE NOTED)

Library of Congress Cataloging-in-Publication Data
Shackelford, Anita.
        Infinite Feathers: quilting designs / Anita Shackelford
            p.   cm.
        ISBN 1-57432-798-4
        1. Quilting--Patterns.   I. Title.
TT835 .S4624 2002
746.46'041--dc21   2002011070

Additional copies of this book may be ordered from the American Quilter's Society, PO Box 3290, Paducah, KY 42002-3290, or online at www.AQSquilt.com.

Acknowledgments

The inspiration to write a book can sometimes begin in mysterious ways. The study of antique quilts, a long-time love of fine hand quilting, the unexpected gift of antique quilting templates ... it would be hard to say which of these had the most important influence on the beginning of this one. As with all the other books I have written, many people have supported my efforts and made contributions along the way. To them I am grateful.

To my family, especially my husband Richard, who patiently shares me with the rest of the world and is always happy when I am home again.

To Meredith Schroeder for her unfailing support of the art of quilting and to the staff at AQS who have made important contributions to this book: Bonnie Browning, Michael Buckingham, Shelley Hawkins, Charles Lynch, Lynda Smith, and Helen Squire.

To the friends who have shared their beautiful quilts and special designs: Liz Carter, Maggie Cunningham, Sharon Finton, Diane Gaudynski, Joan Hipsher, Jane Holihan, Sharon Mareska, Sue Nickels, Andi Perejda, Barb Perrin, Ardie Sveadas, and the International Quilt Study Center.

To my students who continue to enjoy my work and to everyone whose love of feather designs will keep us all quilting.

Contents

Introduction

Feathered designs are among the most elegant quilting patterns. They have been popular since the beginning of quilting history and continue to be used today in traditional and innovative ways.

Believe it or not, feathered designs can be easy to draw. Along with the creative satisfaction, there are many practical advantages in learning to draw your own quilting designs. Rather than depending on commercial stencils in predetermined sizes, you can create designs that fit perfectly in any area of a quilt, regardless of size or shape.

Designing your own quilting patterns is one of the best ways to guarantee that you will have the look you want. It is important that quilting motifs complement the design and mood of the quilt top. When you draw your own designs, you can be as traditional or as fanciful as your heart desires.

Anita Shackelford

Drafting Tips

Quilting patterns can be drawn on paper or directly on the quilt top. If the process of drawing quilting designs is new to you, it is best to draw them on paper first.

The Infinite Feathers template, shown throughout the book, includes 11 cut outs of the teardrop shape in a variety of sizes, and one heart shape. Tracing through the cut-out area makes each feather shape easy to draw and repeat consistently.

A mechanical pencil and eraser are good tools for preliminary drawings. The fine lead of a mechanical pencil allows you to draw close to the edge of the feather cut out, producing the most accurate motif. Have handy a good, soft eraser – one that won't make too many crumbs.

When you are satisfied with a design, trace over the drawing on paper with a dark, permanent marker. This will make the lines easy to see when the pattern is copied onto the quilt top.

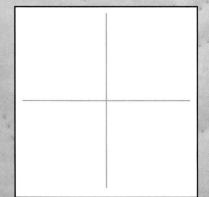

Placement Lines

Some of the feather designs in this book require placement lines for template positioning. For each of these patterns, draw two lines that cross perpendicular to each other. Other placement lines will be added, as needed, based on the complexity of the design.

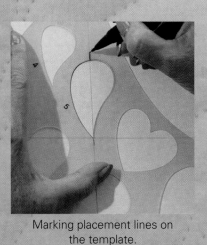

Marking placement lines on
the template.

After the first feather has been drawn, use a pencil to trace the placement line onto the template, above and below the feather cut out. Pencil marks are easily erased from the template when no longer needed.

Anita Shackelford: *Infinite Feathers*

Supplies

Compass or circle guide – Either of these tools can be used for drawing different size centers for feather wreaths. When buying a compass, invest in a quality tool that holds an accurate measurement.

Drawing tools – At minimum, a mechanical pencil, an eraser, and a black fine-line marker are needed for designing on paper. Be sure the marker is permanent on paper so there is no chance of transfer onto the fabric.

Infinite Feathers Quilting Design Template* – This template provides 12 different shapes, plus three curved edges, for drawing many types of feather designs. The cut-out shapes make it easy to see the placement of each feather and to repeat the same feather shape as many times as needed. If you do not have the template, trace the basic feather shape shown in each section and repeat it as necessary to create the design.

Paper – Large sheets of paper are required for the design process and for permanent copies of the designs you intend to keep. Vellum, tracing paper, graph paper, and freezer paper are all helpful at various times.

Protractor – A protractor is used to measure the smaller divisions/radiating lines for more complex designs such as feathered wreaths. Circular grids in a variety of degrees are provided on pages 153–158.

Ruler – A grid ruler with a 45° line is helpful in marking basic placement lines for pinwheels and rosettes.

As you work through the patterns in this book, you may want to add other stencils or templates for drawing hearts, stars, ovals, etc.* These shapes can be used as the center of several designs, or they can be added to feather designs in many different ways.

*See Resources, page 159 for ordering information.

Designing Motifs

The exercises in this section present the steps needed to draw many types of feather designs, progressing from simple shapes to larger, more complex designs. Please try at least one sample of each of the simpler ones before moving to more complex designs or stepping out on your own. Many designs carry over information from a previous style and you will learn important details and gain confidence as you work through each sample.

Pinwheels

Pinwheel designs are created when feathers touch in the center and do not overlap each other. The feathers form a simple cross design. The amount of curve or swirl in the motif depends on the shape of the individual feather. Follow these steps for even placement of the feathers in a pinwheel design.

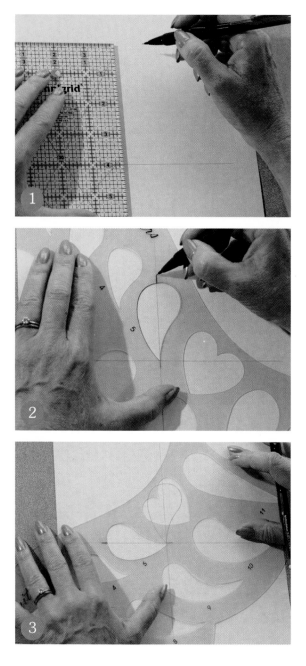

1. Draw the placement lines, page 6.

2. Choose a feather shape and position the template on one of the lines, with the point of the feather touching the intersection of the lines. The feather should stand upright, as shown. Draw one feather. Trace the placement line onto the template.

3. Move the template to the next line, setting the point of the feather at the center. Match the placement lines that were drawn on the template to the line on the paper. Draw the next feather.

4. Repeat the previous step to draw a feather on the two remaining lines.

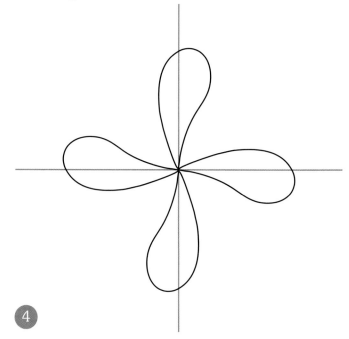

Be Creative! Pinwheels

- Add a larger feather or two behind the first one to create a double- or triple-feather pinwheel.

- Use the heart template in place of a feather to create the Four Hearts design.

Double-Feather Pinwheel

Triple-Feather Pinwheel

Four Hearts Pinwheel

Rosettes

Like pinwheels, rosette designs are drawn with an upright placement of individual feathers. However, in this design, the motif usually includes a center circle. By dividing the design space into smaller sections, more feathers can be added to the basic pinwheel shape, creating a motif with a flower-petal look. Depending on the size of the feather chosen, the feathers may or may not overlap as they repeat around the design.

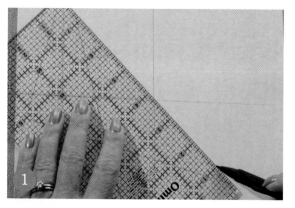

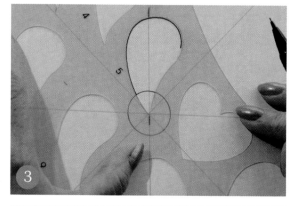

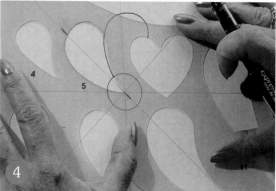

1. Draw the placement lines, page 6. Use a grid ruler or protractor to add diagonal lines through the center of the placement lines in both directions at the 45° points. If you are using a ruler, position it so the 45° line is on one of the pencil lines and the edge of the ruler crosses through the center point.

2. Add a small center circle to the placement lines with a compass or circle guide.

3. Choose a feather motif and position it almost upright on the line, with the point touching the center where the placement lines cross. Draw the feather, omitting the lines that fall behind the circle. Trace the placement line onto the template.

4. With the placement lines on the paper as a guide, draw a feather in the same position on each line. Notice that when feathers overlap, only part of the template is traced. Advance the template in a counter-clockwise direction to draw feathers on the remaining lines. Draw only the full outer curve of the feather and stop when the line of the new feather touches the shoulder of the previous one.

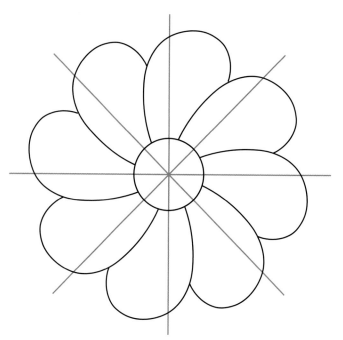

Anita Shackelford: *Infinite Feathers*

Be Creative! Rosettes

Alter the design of the rosette by changing the size of the center circle, eliminating the center circle, drawing the heart template instead of the feather, or alternating heart and feather motifs.

Rosette with Larger Center

No Center Circle

Hearts

Hearts & Feathers

Classic Feathered Wreaths

One of the most frequently used and beloved feather designs is the feathered wreath. Compared to the rosette, feathered wreath designs generally include a larger center circle and more feathers. The placement of the feather and angle of attachment are different from the rosette as well.

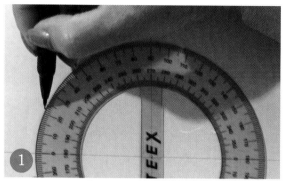

Mark every 22.5° around the half circle.

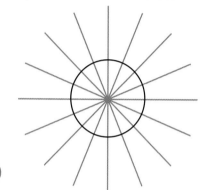

Trace a portion of the circle onto the template.

1. Draw the placement lines, page 6. Center a protractor over the lines, with the 0°–180° marks on the horizontal line and the 90° mark on the vertical line. Make small marks every 22.5° around the half circle. Remove the protractor.

2. Draw a line that connects each degree mark to the center. Continue each line through the center to draw placement lines for the lower half of the design. Add a 5" center circle with a compass or circle guide. The circle should be one-third to one-half the size of the space to be filled.

3. Use the #3 feather motif and position it so the point touches the circle and the feather is at an angle, as shown. Draw the feather. Trace the placement lines onto the template. Tracing a portion of the center circle provides an additional guide.

4. With the placement lines on the paper as a guide, draw a feather motif in the same position on each line.

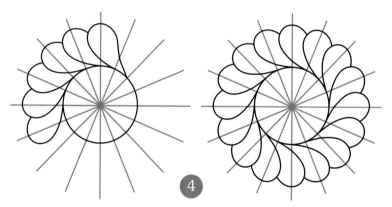

Feather Overlap

The amount of overlap of the feathers can be varied by changing the number of degrees in the repeat. Varying the number of feathers in the same size wreath creates different looks.

- Advancing the template so the full shape of the feather is shown produces a soft petal effect.

- A slight overlap creates a traditional feather look.

- A tight overlap creates a full, rich look.

Be Creative! Feathered Wreaths

- Draw a double-feathered wreath, with feathers on the outside and inside of the spine. When drawing the inside feathers, the angle of placement needs to be tighter, nearly parallel to the spine. As a general rule, only half as many feathers are needed to fill the inner space. You can do this simply by placing a feather on every other positioning line.

- Place larger feathers in the corners to change the look of the wreath and create a design that fills a square block more completely.

Template placement for inside feathers.

Double-Feathered Wreath

Larger Feathers in Corners

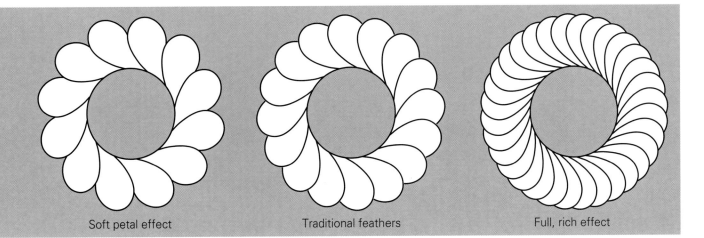

Soft petal effect

Traditional feathers

Full, rich effect

Be Creative! Center Medallions

Wreaths and rosettes can be drawn to fill large areas, such as the center medallion of an Amish-style quilt or whole-cloth designs. These medallions require large center circles, large feather shapes, and close repeats. Follow the instructions in Classic Feathered Wreaths, page 12, to draw these designs and use small divisions such as 10° or 12° when drawing the placement lines.*

• Large wreaths can include a single or a double spine. The centers can be filled with parallel lines, grids, more feathers, or other motifs such as a star or rosette.

• A Perfect Spiral pattern is beautiful in an open center and can be drawn according to the degree lines that are already in place.

Grid Quilting in Center

Star Motif in Center

Perfect Spiral Pattern in Center

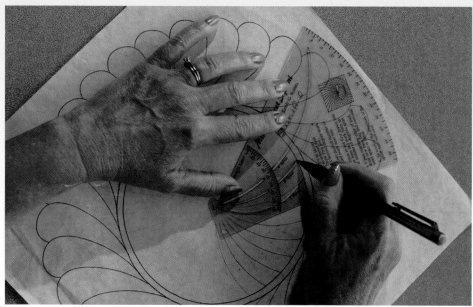

Perfect Spiral template placement. See Resources, page 159 for ordering information.

*For more information on drafting large wreaths, see Designing to Fit the Space, page 33.

Ovals

When a circular center is changed to an oval shape, feathers can be drawn in mirror image rather than in a continuous pattern.

1. Draw a vertical line in the center of the design space. With a template, draw an oval shape one-fourth to one-third the size of the space to be filled, or copy the shape in the pattern section, page 86. Position the first feather at the top of the oval, with the pointed end touching the oval spine and the plume curling up to touch the center line. If you are left-handed, you will probably find it easier to flip the template and draw feathers on the left side of the design.

2. Advance the template along the outside of the spine, drawing feathers that overlap in a pleasing manner. Stop one feather short of the bottom. Study the feather placement and decide if any feathers need to be moved in or out a little to create a more pleasing shape. The spacing of the feathers should be uniform. Make adjustments, if needed.

3. Fold the paper in half on the center line and trace the feathers to create the other half of the design. Open the paper and add a motif at the bottom to fill the remaining space.

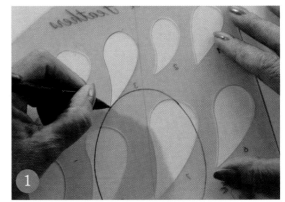

Left-handed template placement.

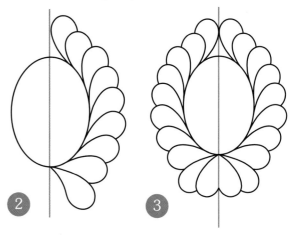

Be Creative! Ovals

- Change the size of the oval. Try a design with a smaller center and large feathers, or a large center and small feathers.

- Change the shape of the center, as in the pineapple variation.

- Consider different design options for the motif at the bottom, such as a single teardrop, double feathers, a heart, or larger feathers for a wide base. Look at designs in the Pattern section, pages 85–88 for inspiration.

Small Oval with Large Feathers

Feathered Pineapple

Feathered Oval with Heart Motif

Hearts

Like ovals, feathered hearts repeat their shape side to side, making them perfectly balanced and visually pleasing.

1. Draw a vertical line in the center of the design space. Use a template or draw freehand to create a spine for half of a heart design.

2. Begin by drawing feathers at the bottom of the heart, or choose an additional motif to reverse the pattern, such as a single teardrop feather, a pair of curved feathers, or a smaller heart.

3. Advance the template along the outside of the spine, drawing feathers that overlap in a pleasing manner.

4. Before reaching the top, decide how you want the pattern to finish. The feathers may or may not touch, or they might finish in a deep curl. Because the image mirrors itself, it will be pleasing any way you choose. Draw the top feathers. Check the remaining space to see if adjustments are needed in the spacing of the final feathers. A few feathers may have to be repositioned to make it all fit.

5. Fold the paper in half along the center line and copy the design to the other side.

Motifs to reverse the pattern.

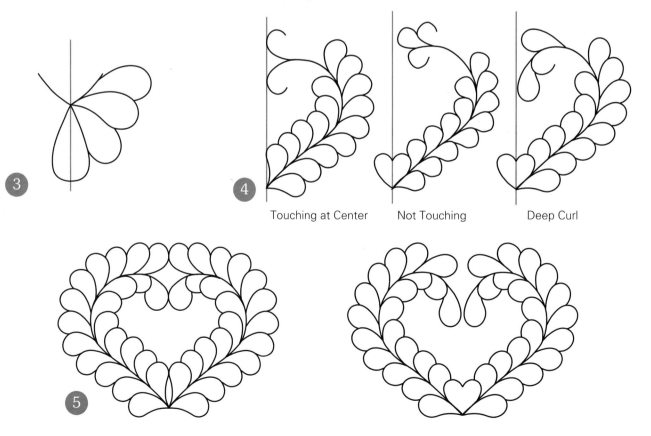

Touching at Center Not Touching Deep Curl

Be Creative! Hearts

- Create a Bleeding Heart design by turning the feathers down instead of up.

- Draw feathers on the inside as well as the outside of the heart.

- Draw a double spine and fill the center with another quilting pattern. Good choices for filling interior spaces include straight lines in vertical and horizontal patterns, double- and triple-line spacing, grid, clamshells, and stipple quilting.

Template placement for Bleeding Heart.

Bleeding Heart

Double-Feathered Heart

Heart with stipple quilting.

Double-Spined Heart with Straight Line Filler

Heart in FEATHER SAMPLER, made by the author.

Lyres

The lyre is another design that is drawn with side-to-side symmetry.

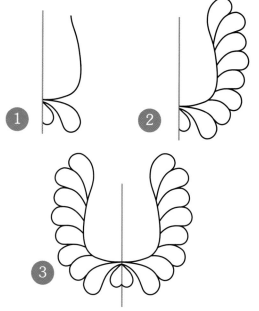

1. Draw a vertical line in the center of the design space. Draw half of the spine for the lyre. Think of it as half of a "U" shape, wider at the bottom, or perhaps a slight "S" shape, curving to the outside at the top. Choose a pattern for the bottom of the motif, such as the #10 feather on the template and a small heart. Draw the first feather.

2. Advance the template along the outside of the spine, drawing feathers that overlap in a pleasing manner. Extend the final feather at the top to create a visually pleasing tip.

3. Fold the paper in half along the center line and copy the design to the other side.

Be Creative! Lyres

- Draw a double-feather design, with feathers inside and out.

- Combine different feather sizes to create an exciting look.

- Finish the motif with a bar and strings for a traditional lyre design.

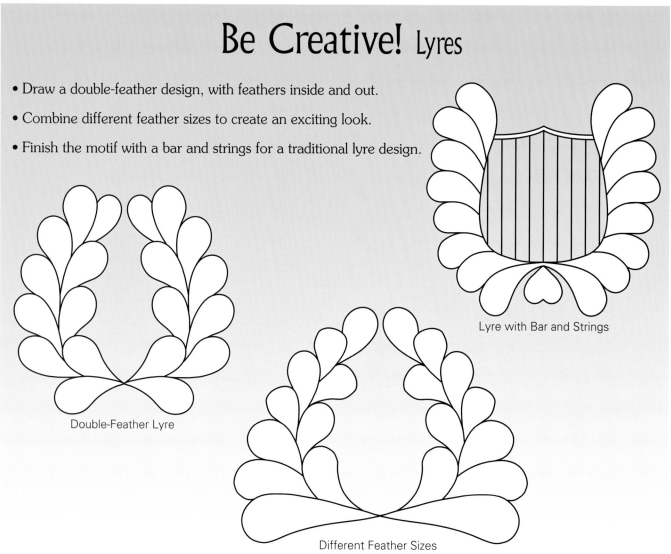

Lyre with Bar and Strings

Double-Feather Lyre

Different Feather Sizes

Plumes

Plumes can be symmetrical or asymmetrical designs, drawn to follow a straight or curved spine. The spine can be single, double, open, or eliminated.

Symmetrical

1. Draw a straight line the desired length of the motif. Begin with a single feather, positioned at the desired angle, at the bottom of the line. Advance the template along the spine, drawing feathers that overlap in a pleasing manner.

2. When you are near the top of the line, fold the paper in half on the center line and copy the feathers to the other side. Add the #1 feather on the top to join the sides.

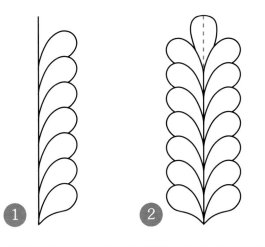

Asymmetrical

1. Draw a curved spine freehand in a relaxed "S" shape. If you prefer a double spine, draw a second line parallel to the first.

2. Choose a feather that is compatible with the size of the spine and the space to be filled. Begin at the bottom and draw feathers along one side of the spine. Note that the feathers on the inside curve will be slightly shortened and lie close to the spine, while those on the outside curve should be longer and lean farther away from the spine.

3. Flip the template and draw feathers along the other side of the spine. The placement of feathers does not have to match from side to side; just give each feather its own space. Fit a final feather into the tip to join the sides. In an asymmetrical design, a curved feather at the end is usually more pleasing than a straight one.

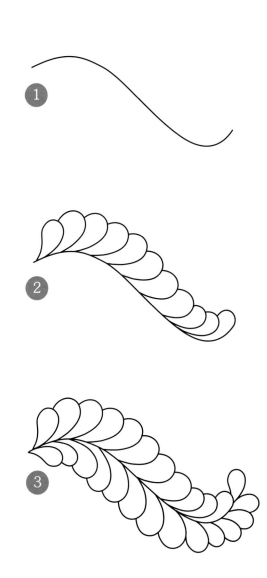

Asymmetrical plume in Coxcomb with Berries, shown on page 57.

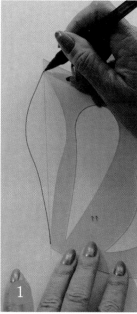

Symmetrical open spine.

Symmetrical with an open spine

1. Trace the curved edge on the side of the template. Flip the template and draw the same curve again, connecting it to the first line at the top and bottom.

2. Begin at the bottom and draw a single feather, positioned at the desired angle. Advance the template along the curve, drawing feathers that overlap in a pleasing manner.

3. When you are near the top, fold the paper in half, matching the open spine lines. Copy the feathers to create the other side of the plume. Use the #1 feather to fill in the tip of the design.

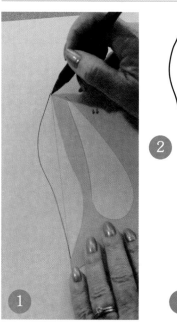

Asymmetrical open spine.

Asymmetrical with an open spine

1. Trace the curved edge on the side of the template. Rotate the template and draw the same curve again, connecting it to the first line at the top and bottom.

2. Choose a feather that is compatible with the size of the overall design. Begin at the bottom and draw feathers along one side of the spine.

3. Flip the template and draw feathers along the other side of the spine. Fit a final feather into the top to join the sides. In an asymmetrical design, a curved feather at the tip is usually more pleasing than a straight one.

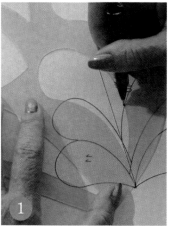

Draw feathers alternately on the right and left sides of the line.

No spine

1. Draw a line as a guide for the length and curve of the plume. Beginning at the bottom, draw feathers alternately on the right and left sides of the line. Position the template so that successive feathers overlap each other and overlap the center line slightly to create an interesting, braided pattern.

2. Alternate feathers side to side, or position a few more toward the outside curve. Add a final feather to join the sides at the tip of the design.

Anita Shackelford: *Infinite Feathers*

Be Creative! Plumes

- Draw a Fiddlehead design with a tightly curled top, similar to a question mark, and add feathers on only one side.

- Add a heart instead of a single feather at the top of the design.

- Try a design with large feathers on one side, and small feathers on the other.

Fiddlehead Plume with
Feathers Outside

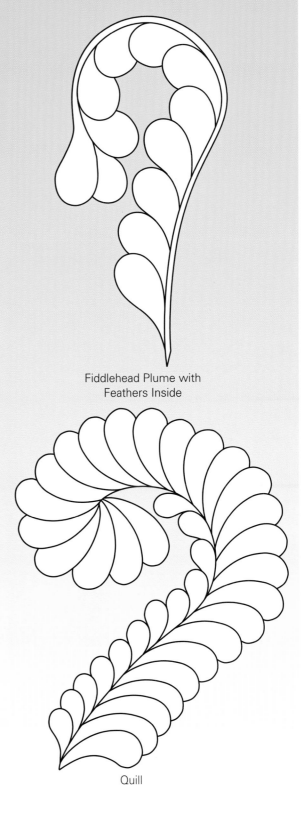

Fiddlehead Plume with
Feathers Inside

Heart-Tipped Plume

Quill

Paisleys

Paisley designs are larger motifs with feathers drawn around a paisley-shaped center or a similar asymmetrical shape.

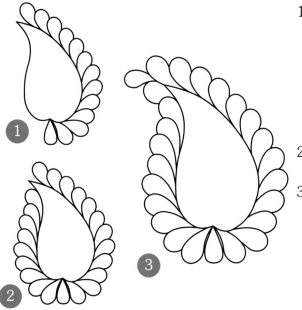

1. Draw or trace a paisley motif for the center of the design. See the Pattern section, pages 102–109, for a variety of paisley shapes. Choose a motif that will reverse the pattern at the bottom of the design, such as a heart or a single teardrop. Add feathers along one side, stopping one or two feathers short of the top.

2. Flip the template and add feathers to the other side.

3. Finish the design by adding feathers to alternate sides, merging them into a pleasing pattern at the tip.

Be Creative! Paisleys

- Draw feathers around only part of the design. The change adds visual interest to the motif and there is no need to match the pattern from one side to the other.

- The interior space of paisleys can be filled with a variety of patterns, including straight lines in vertical and horizontal patterns, double- and triple-line spacing, grid, clamshells, and stipple quilting.

Partial-Feathered Paisley

Clamshell-Filled Paisley

Peacock Feathers

Peacock Feather motifs are attractive groupings of feathers without a spine. The feathers spread from a common base point to make a fan shape, which can fill the space of a quarter-circle to a half-circle. Peacock Feathers fit nicely in triangular spaces and background corners, such as the corners of a Dresden Plate block.

Symmetrical

1. Draw a baseline and a vertical center line for feather placement. Draw the first feather, positioned to touch the vertical line.

2. Rotate the template and continue to add feathers for half of the design. The pointed end of all the feathers should touch the same base point.

3. Fold the paper in half on the center line and copy the feathers to the other side. Add the #1 feather to the center, if desired.

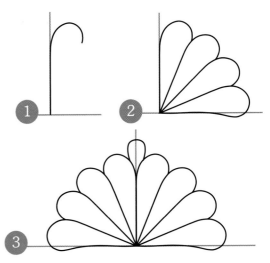

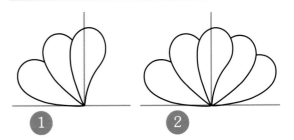

Asymmetrical I

1. Draw a baseline and a vertical center line. Draw a feather, positioned on the vertical center line. Add a feather or two on one side, as needed, to fill the space.

2. Flip the template and add one or two feathers to the other side.

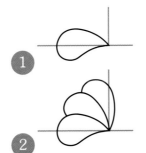

Asymmetrical II

1. Draw a baseline and a vertical center line. Position a feather on the baseline.

2. Rotate the template and add successive feathers to create a full fan shape.

Peacock Feathers in Dresden Plate block, made by the author.

Be Creative! Peacock Feathers

- Choose a different shape for the center of the motif.

- Combine different sizes of feathers within the same motif.

Different Shaped Center   Different Feather Sizes

Swags

A swag is a symmetrical design that follows a curved line, with the center draping downward from the two end points. It can be used as a single motif in a specific place, in combination to fill a large space, or repeated to fill a border.

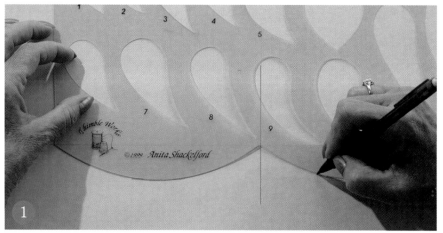

Trace the lower edge of the template to draw a spine.

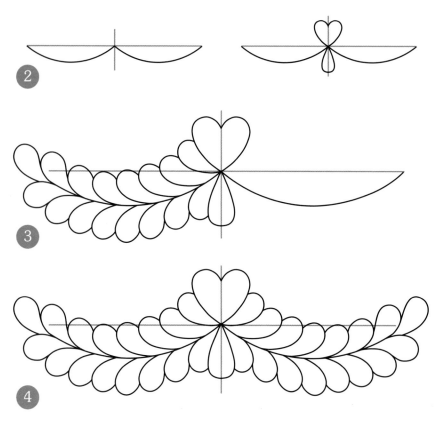

1. Draw a baseline and a vertical center line. Trace the curved, lower edge of the template to draw a spine for the swag design. If you prefer a double spine, trace the edge of the template a second time. Both ends and the center of the curved spine should touch the baseline.

2. Add a heart at the top and the #1 feather at the bottom center of the curved spine. These symmetrical shapes will reverse the flow of feathers along the spine.

3. Add feathers above and below the spine on one side. After the first feather is drawn, trace a part of the curved spine onto the template. Use this line to help position successive feathers along the spine. Add a final feather at the tip of the spine.

4. Fold the paper in half on the center line and copy the feathers to the other side.

Swag in FEATHER SAMPLER, made by the author.

Be Creative! Swags

- Try other center motifs to reverse the flow of the design.

- Use a combination of feather sizes to add interest to the design.

- Connect several swags by adding feathers that merge into a single, joining motif.

- Reverse the swag to create a spine that arches up instead of draping down.

Different Center Motif

Different Sizes of Feathers

Continuous Feather Swag

Arching Swag

Borders

Feathers for border designs can be placed along a straight or curved spine. Subtract the seam allowance and the width of the binding when calculating the size of the design space in a border.

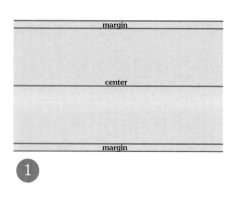

Straight spine

1. Draw a section of the border on paper. Measure the width of the border to find the center. Add a straight line for the center spine. Draw margin lines ¼" inside each edge as a guide for usable design space.

2. Measure the length of the border and mark the spacing along the spine to ensure even placement of feathers. In this example, feathers were placed every 1" along the spine. A more suitable spacing for smaller feathers might be ¾".

3. Choose a feather that fits in the space between the center line and the margin line. Draw the first feather. Advance the template to the next mark on the center line, making sure that the curve touches the outside margin line. Draw the second feather. Repeat to fill the length of the border on one side.

4. Fold the paper in half along the center line and copy to repeat identical feather placement on the opposite side.

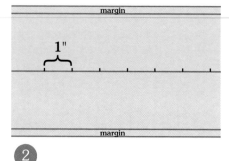

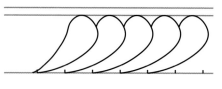

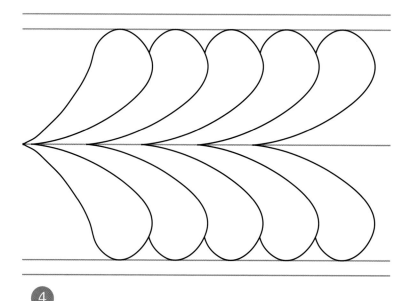

Be Creative! Borders

- You can produce slight variations in the final width of a design based on the angle at which the feather meets the spine. With the same feather, a perpendicular placement creates a wider border, while a feather placed at a tighter angle produces a slightly narrower design.

- A rosette center and a straight spine running in both directions can be extended and repeated to fill a border.

- Consider using the seam line as a straight spine, and draw feathers along one edge of the border.

WELSH HEART, shown on page 58.

Straight Feathered Border

Rosette-Centered Border

Feathered Border along the Seam Line

Curved spine

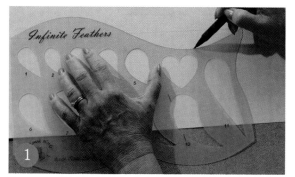

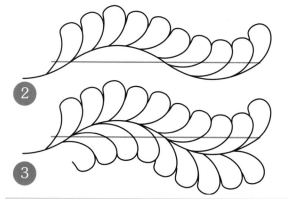

Trace the edge of the template.

The Infinite Feathers template has a long, curved edge that can be traced to create a spine for undulating feather designs.

1. Draw a section of the border on paper. Add a line through the center of the border. Draw margin lines ¼" inside each border edge as a guide for usable design space. Position the template with the corners touching the center line, and trace the edge of the template.

2. Draw feathers along one side of the spine, with feathers on the outside curve somewhat upright, and those on the inside curve closer to the spine.

3. Draw feathers along the other side of the spine. Do not try to draw the feathers in pairs. Feathers that flow along inside and outside curves will not match across the spine as they do in a straight border.

Be Creative! Borders

- Change the spacing or the amount of overlap of the feathers.
- Draw a double-overlap spine.

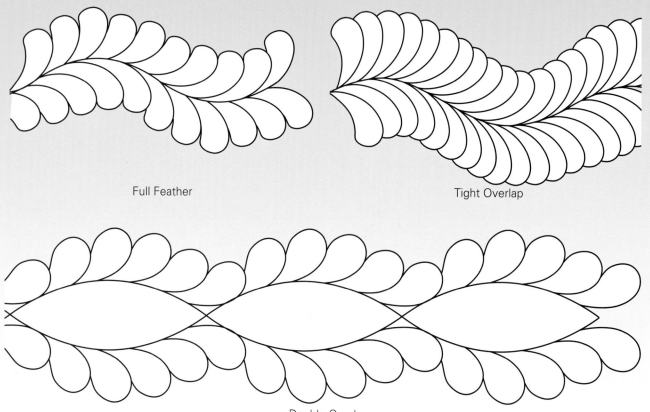

Full Feather

Tight Overlap

Double Overlap

Anita Shackelford: *Infinite Feathers*

Be Creative! Borders

- Draw a double spine by positioning the template with the corners slightly above the center line, and an equal space below the line. The width of a double spine should be based on the size of the feathers and the overall scale of the design. Make a progressive change in the size of the feathers along the spine by placing large feathers on the inside curve and smaller feathers on the outside.

- Draw feathers only on the inside of a deeply curved spine that almost touches the seam line as it undulates along the border.

- Draw a feathered border, leaving bare areas along the spine.

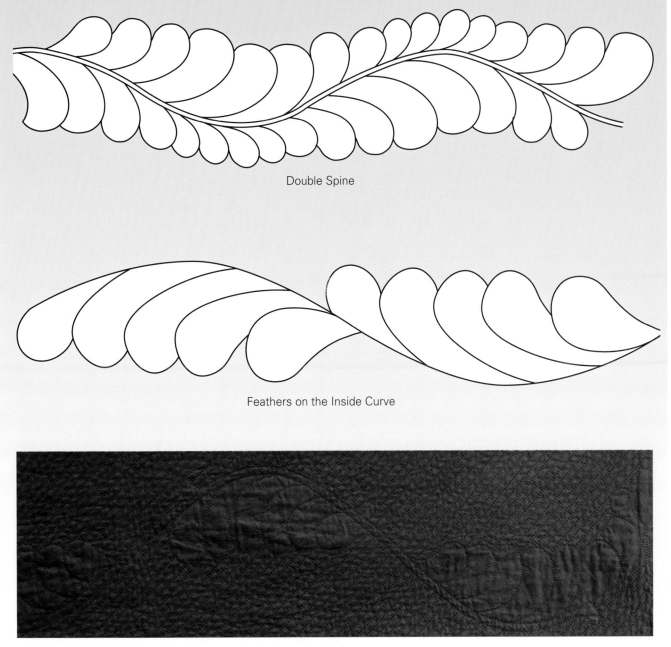

Double Spine

Feathers on the Inside Curve

Bare areas along the spine in a border hand quilted by the author.

Combining Designs

Some of the designs in the previous section, such as plumes and swags, can be combined to fill large spaces. Motifs can be mirrored or multiplied in several different ways to create designs that are perfect choices for the large, open blocks in alternate sets, or as center medallions.

Some of these designs require a reverse image, which can be made on a copy machine, computer, or by hand. With tracing paper and a light box, you can see and position several images at the same time.

Doubles

Mirrored Plumes

Begin this design by copying a reverse image of a favorite asymmetrical plume. Depending on the shape of the plume, the mirror-image combination will make a heart, a pineapple, or another symmetrical design. With minor adjustments, the design can be open or closed at the top. Play with the design a little until you find the perfect fit.

Crossed Plumes

Another design that can be made with a repeated motif is a pair of crossed plumes. To create this design, lay one motif across the other and adjust the angle to find a pleasing design that fits the space.

Quads

Four repeats are the most frequently used combination because they fit perfectly in a square block of any size. Begin by drawing the full-size block on paper. Add lines from corner to corner to divide the block into quadrants. Find the center of each side of the block and draw lines connecting these points to divide the block into eighths. These divisions are helpful for any design that repeats four or eight times.

Symmetrical

1. Divide the full-size block into eighths, as previously described.

2. Choose a favorite symmetrical plume and draw one plume on each of the four lines, extending from the center to the corners of the block. Be sure that the individual feathers do not extend beyond the quadrant lines into the design space of the next one. Make adjustments or add feathers as necessary so the center design is pleasing.

Asymmetrical

An asymmetrical motif, such as the feather curl shown here, can be an interesting way to fill four quadrants in a block. Follow the previous steps for drawing a symmetrical quad, substituting an asymmetrical plume. For a successful repeat, choose a motif that fills most of the design space.

Peacock Feathers

Four Peacock Feather motifs, placed in the corners of a block, leave an open center, making it suitable to use as a frame around an appliquéd motif. The center area can also be filled with a quilted grid or other design.

1. Divide the full-size block into eighths.

2. Draw a Peacock Feather motif centered on each placement line that extends into a corner. Peacock Feather designs are most pleasing if the sides of the motifs touch each other as they repeat around the block.

Swags

Symmetrical feathered swags, repeated four times, create beautiful, classic patterns for large blocks. This pattern also has an open center that can be filled with a quilted grid or other design.

1. Divide the full-size block into eighths.

2. Draw a swag design across a corner or along the side of the block. Be sure that the motif is centered on the placement line and that the ends of the swag just touch the lines for the next section. The swag itself can be positioned to drape into the block or out toward the sides.

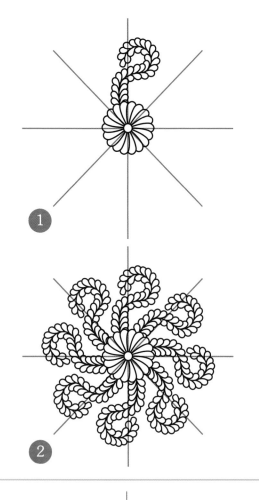

Eights
Eight Plumes

Eight repeats create the largest combination designs, perfect for medallion centers. A plume repeated eight times produces a Princess Feather-type design.

1. Divide the full-size block into eighths. Position a plume on top of the divided block. Move the plume away from the center, as needed, to prevent it from overlapping the adjacent design space. Trace the placement line through the center of the plume motif.

2. Reverse the position so the plume is underneath the block. Match the placement lines and trace one plume onto each line to create a design with eight repeats. Draw a pretty rosette or feathered wreath for a center focus.

Eight Hearts

Symmetrical feathered hearts, placed in a circle, create a different look. When the bottom points almost meet in the center, they form a star in the negative space.

1. Divide the full-size block into eighths. Choose a narrow feathered heart motif and place it under the divided block. Center the heart on one of the placement lines. Move the heart away from the center of the design space, as needed, to prevent it from overlapping the adjacent space. Trace one heart on each line to create a design with eight repeats.

2. Add lines, as shown, to create an eight-pointed star in the center.

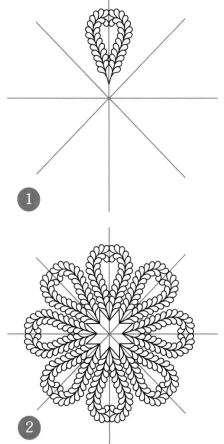

Designing to Fit the Space

Blocks

When you are ready to draft a design for a specific space in your quilt, begin by drawing the full-size block on paper. Draw margin lines inside the seam lines to establish the usable design space. Small blocks need a ¼" margin from the seam line, making the finished size of the design approximately ½" smaller than the block size. Large blocks look more pleasing with a ⅜" to ½" margin all around.

Feathered Wreaths

1. Draw the full-size block on paper. Add margin lines to determine the finished size of the wreath. Place a ruler corner to corner in each direction, and make a small mark to find the center of the block. Add a horizontal line through the center. Draw a center circle, approximately one-half to three-quarters the size of the block. Choose a feather that fills the space between the center circle and the margin line. Draw the first feather on the line. Before moving the template, copy the positioning line onto the template, above and below the feather cut out.

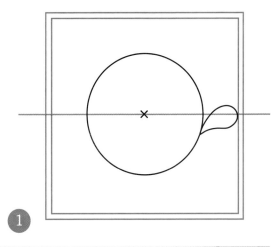

2. Advance the template to find the approximate placement for the next feather. Place a protractor in the center of the design space, with the zero mark on the line. Place a ruler over both the protractor and the template. The edge of the ruler should cross the center mark, and extend to align with the placement lines on the template. Read the protractor to find the number of degrees for the next placement line. It is important that the number of degrees in each step divide equally into 360°.

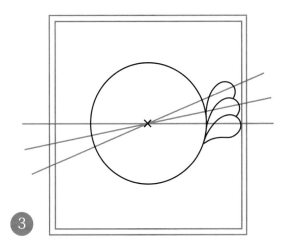

Place a ruler over both the protractor and the template to find the number of degrees for the next placement.

3. Use the protractor and the calculated number of degrees to measure and mark the desired spacing around the top half of the design. With a ruler and mechanical pencil, draw a line connecting each measurement mark to the center. Continue each line through the center to draw placement lines for the lower half of the circle. Draw feathers on each line to complete the motif.

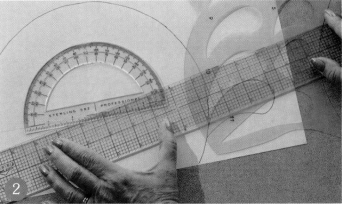

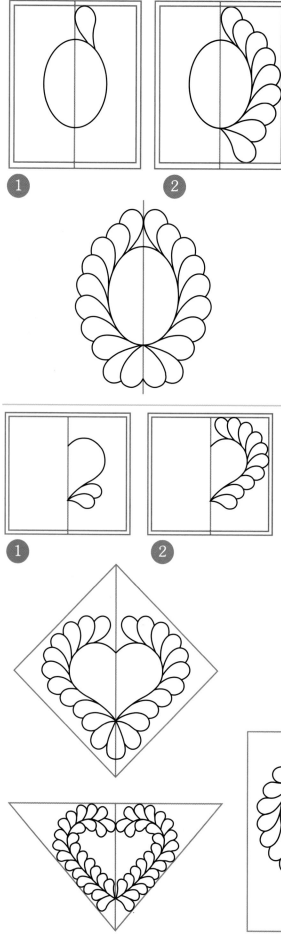

Rectangles

Ovals, paisleys, and lyres are good choices to fill rectangular blocks. The size of each center shape can vary, but the proportions (length and width) of the center should be similar to those of the block.

1. Draw the full-size block on paper. Add margin lines to determine the design space.

2. Draw a vertical center line. Choose a center shape and draw it on the line. Add feathers in the sizes needed to create a design that fills the space.

Feathered Hearts

Feathered hearts are amazingly versatile. The size and shape of a heart can be stretched, squeezed, or pulled into proportions that fit a block set square or on-point, a horizontal or vertical rectangle, or a triangle.

1. Draw the full-size block on paper. Add margin lines to determine the design space.

2. Draw a vertical center line. The placement of this line will depend on the shape of the space to be filled. Draw half of a heart shape, keeping in mind the proportions of the block. Trace a feather or combination of feathers to create a design that fills the space.

Anita Shackelford: *Infinite Feathers*

Triangles

When quilt blocks are set on-point, there is sometimes a need for quilting designs to fill a triangular block. Visually, these motifs are more pleasing if they are designed to fit the space and not simply cut off at the seam line.

Symmetrical

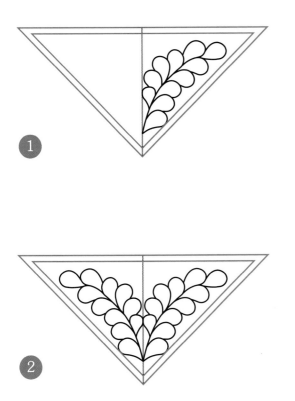

1. Draw the outside dimensions of the finished triangle. Draw margin lines ¼" inside each edge as a guide for usable design space. Add a center line that runs from the square corner to the center of the long side. Draw a spine that begins in the square corner and flows out to the side. Choose a feather size that is compatible with the space to be filled. Begin in the corner, leaving a ¼" to ½" margin, and draw feathers along one side of the spine. Flip the template and draw feathers along the other side, being careful not to cross the center line of the triangle. Add a final feather at the end, leaving an adequate margin at the seam line.

2. Fold the paper in half on the center line and trace the design to the other side.

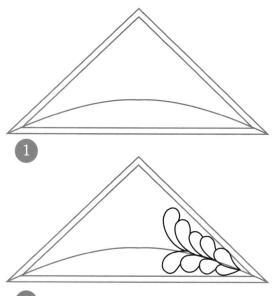

Asymmetrical

1. Draw the outside dimensions of the finished triangle. Add margin lines. Draw a curved spine that runs from narrow corner to narrow corner.

2. Beginning at one end, draw feathers alternately, above and below the spine. Use a combination of sizes to fill the space. Position the template so that successive feathers overlap each other and overlap the center line slightly to create an interesting pattern in the center.

3. Alternate feathers side to side, or position a few more toward the outside curve.

Extend feathers, as necessary, to fill the space.

Borders

There are several ways to design a border that fits the quilt. Each of the following works well; however, the circumstance and your preferred method of working may determine your choice.

Pattern Repeats

No matter what style of border pattern you choose, it is important to match the position of the first feather in each repeat so the pattern can be joined and the feathers flow in a continuous design.

1. Draw a center line. Trace the edge of the template to draw an undulating spine, creating one repeat.

2. Add small lines to mark the beginning and end of the repeat. Draw feathers above and below the spine, stopping several feathers short of one full repeat.

3. Roll the paper end to end, matching pattern repeats, so the beginning and the end of the baseline touch. Trace the beginning of the pattern, the first top and bottom feathers, to create the beginning of the second repeat.

4. Open the paper and add feathers to fill in the gap, making any necessary adjustments in the spacing. The border pattern drawn in this way will connect and flow in a continuous pattern, no matter how many times it is repeated.

Trace the top edge of the template to draw an undulating spine.

Roll the paper end to end, matching pattern repeats, and trace the first feathers.

Lines mark the beginning and end of one pattern repeat.

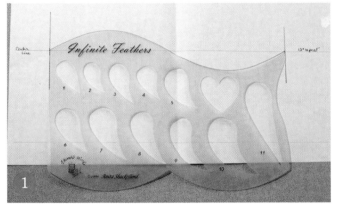

Finished repeat.

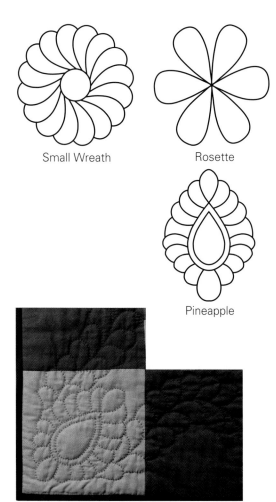

Small Wreath

Rosette

Pineapple

Corner motif hand quilted by the author.

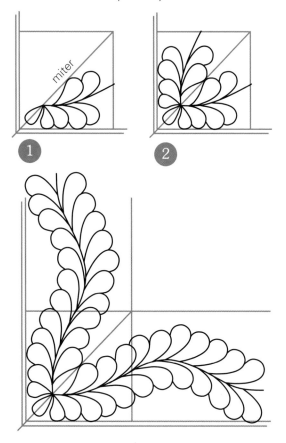

Corner Options

There are many options for filling the corners of a quilt with a feather border. A border pattern can end at the seam line, and the corner block can be filled with an independent motif. Border designs can flow from the corners and fill the borders with a pattern that meets in the middle, or they can turn the corner in a continuous pattern.

Separate corner motif

One of the simplest ways to handle the corner of a border pattern is to interrupt the flow of the design with a separate corner motif. Old-Order Amish quilts were pieced with corner blocks to connect the borders, and the quilting designs often followed the same format. A corner motif is a good choice for a traditional or folk-art quilt, which includes corner blocks. This idea works as well in new designs. Shown here are examples of good corner motifs, including a small wreath, rosette, and pineapple.

Design from the corner

One way to ensure that the border design fits the corner is to draft a pattern that begins there.

1. Draw a block the size of the corner square and mark a miter line. Place a mark where the border spine will begin. Draw a feather design on half of the block, keeping in mind how it will connect to the border design.

2. Fold the paper in half on the miter line and trace the design to the other side to create a symmetrical motif. Extend the spine, as desired, for a straight or undulating feather design.

Because this type of mirror-image motif forces the border design to flow from the corner to the center of each border, draw a design that fills approximately half of the border length. Make adjustments in the center of the border where the two designs meet. You can leave a small open space, merge the feathers into a new design, or join the designs with a completely different motif. See page 42 for more ideas on joining patterns in the middle of the border.

Design into the corner

Another option is to draw the design so it runs into the corner instead of away from it. This type of design begins with a motif in the center of the border and merges in the corner.

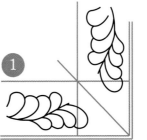

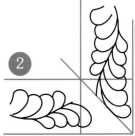

1. Begin the running design in the center of the border. Draw feathers, as desired, stopping a few inches short of the corner. Mark a miter line through the corner block.

2. Extend the spine into half of the corner block, so the pattern flows in a pleasing manner. Add feathers to the spine, being careful not to cross the miter line.

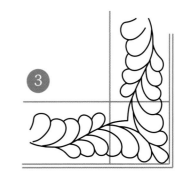

3. Fold the paper on the miter line and copy the pattern to the other side. Add a final feather to join the two sides of the design

Design around the corner

1. Draw the corner square. Mark a miter line, as well as the position where the border spines touch the sides of the block.

2. Extend the spine from one side of the block to the miter line.

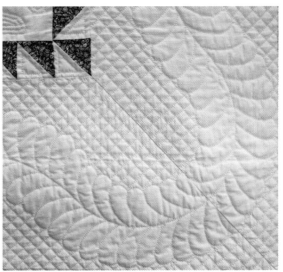

3. Fold the paper in half and copy the spine to the other side. Open the paper to see if the spine flows as desired before continuing. Add feathers to begin the new pattern at the far side of the corner block. The placement of these feathers should match the first feathers of the full border pattern.

4. Add more feathers, as needed, to fill the remaining space around the corner.

Continuous feather border in CUTWORK APPLIQUÉ, hand quilted by the author.

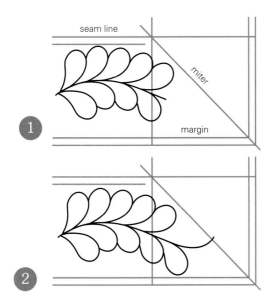

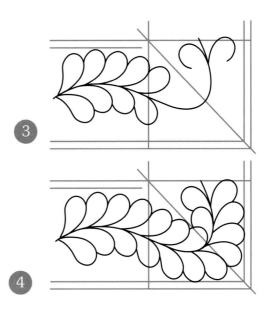

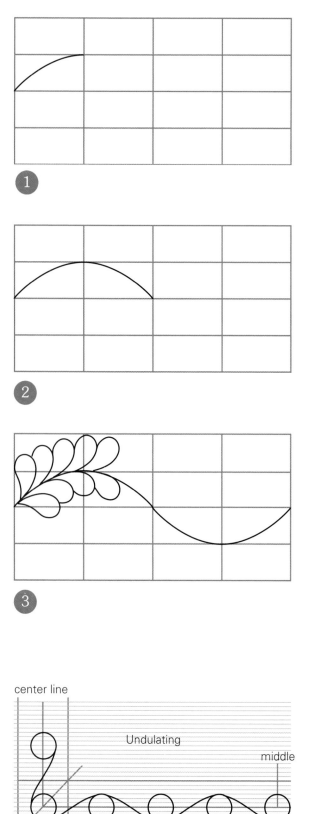

Measured Repeats

You can draft a border that will fit perfectly by working with graph paper and following these steps to draw an undulating spine. Divide the border length (minus the corner) by an odd number, such as 5. For example, an 80" border divided by 5 equals 16". This is the length of a full up-and-down repeat. The odd number of repeats is necessary for the pattern to repeat the same way at each corner.

1. On graph paper, draw a rectangle the width of the border and the length of the repeat. Divide the rectangle into four parts, both vertically and horizontally. Draw a curve that begins on the second horizontal line and extends to the first line, across the first section, as shown. Check the width from the spine to the margin line to be sure there is room for the desired feather. Adjust the curve, if necessary.

2. Fold the paper and copy this line to the second section.

3. Copy the reverse curve into the remaining two sections to create the second half of an undulating spine. Draw feathers on both sides of the spine. Be sure to create a matching pattern at the beginning and end.

When you are ready to transfer the pattern to the quilt, you can work with a single repeat rather than draw a full-length pattern. Measure and mark off sections of the border, and transfer the pattern to each section

No-Math Method

This method offers a hands-on approach, creating a full-size pattern to fit any quilt.

Undulating

- On paper longer than half the length of one border, including the corner, mark a center line in the border and a miter line in the corner. Mark the middle of the border length.

- Draw circles one-third to one-half as wide as the border, placing one in the corner, one in the middle, and the others at evenly spaced intervals. Smaller circles and/or wider spacing create a gently undulating pattern, while larger circles and closer spacing create a serpentine design.

- Draw a flowing line above and below the circles to create an undulating spine that fits the length of the border perfectly. The spine should cross the center line of the border at a point exactly between the two circles. Add feathers along the spine to create the desired pattern.

Curling

Instead of a spine that undulates, follow these steps to draw a line that curls back on itself. Curl patterns generally flow from the corner to the center of each border.

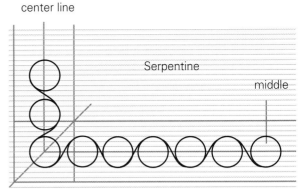

- On paper longer than half the length of the border, including one corner, mark a center line in the border and a miter line in the corner. Mark the middle of the border length.

- Draw circles half as wide as the border, placing one in the corner and a number of others at evenly spaced intervals along the border. Do not place a circle in the middle of the border. The spacing between circles should be the same size as the diameter of the circles, or smaller.

- Draw a flowing line from one circle, curling around the next circle to create a spine. The spine should cross the center line of the border at a point exactly between the two circles. Alternate the pattern to add a spine that curls above one circle and below the next until reaching the middle of the border. Curls in the middle of the pattern will mirror each other.

Adjustments in the Design

If you are working with a border design in a predetermined size and don't want to redraft it, you may be able to adjust the way the design comes together. The following are several other ways to make a continuous border fit.

Individual motifs

Individual motifs, such as swags, can be repeated as many times as necessary to fill a border. Measure the length of the border to find the number of repeats that will fit. The double swag edge on the template measures 12". Feathers can extend from the tip of the spine at each end. The length of these two feathers can be changed to make minor adjustments in the length of one repeat.

Curling feather border in FRIENDSHIP, made by Sharon Mareska, Toledo, Ohio.

Repeated swag in FEATHER SAMPLER, made by the author.

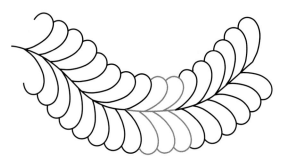

Adjust to Fill Small Gap

You can also draw a preliminary design at 12", and then enlarge or reduce the entire design to fit. Or, you can make adjustments in the spacing between the individual motifs to ensure that it comes out even. Many other individual motifs can be repeated at measured intervals to fill any size border.

Running borders

If a running border design almost fits, it is usually possible to join the border by simply adding or removing a feather or two in the middle of the design.

When a design runs from the corner, the pattern is adjusted in the middle of the border. If there is a small gap in the design, consider adding another design element, or continue each pattern and merge the designs in the center. A large gap can be filled by allowing each spine to curl back on itself. Curls in mirror image will form a pleasing design in the center of each border. If the spines almost meet in the middle but are offset top and bottom, consider allowing them to curl around each other.

Merged Designs

Spines Curling Back

Spines Curling around Each Other

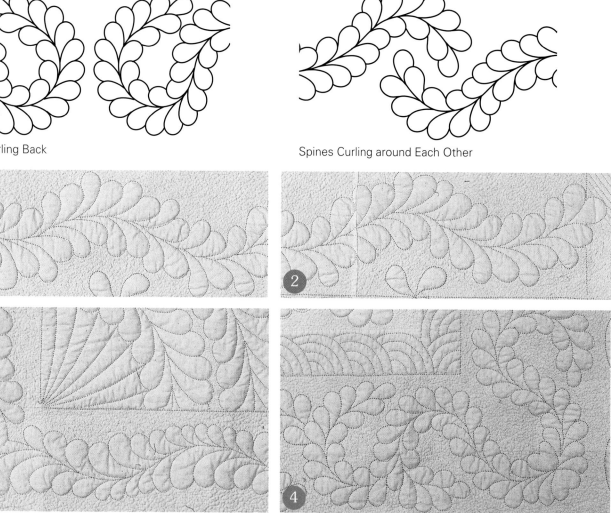

Borders in FEATHER SAMPLER, made by the author. Photos 1. and 2. running border, 3. feather corner, 4. curling border.

Continuous-Line Designs

If you plan to quilt feathers by machine, continuous-line designs are the easiest patterns because there is only one point in the design where the stitching starts and stops. A pinwheel, where every feather comes together in the center, is a perfect example. You can begin stitching in the center, stitch around each feather, and finish where you started. Tie the thread ends together, pull them into the quilt, and the design is finished.

Feathered wreaths can be drawn with each feather touching a portion of the center circle, but with the feathers isolated from each other. To draft a continuous-line feathered wreath, follow the same steps on page 12. Measure with a protractor to find the number of degrees that will cause a slight separation between the feathers, rather than an overlap. Any size or shape of feather can be used in this pattern. Running borders can be designed in the same way by advancing the template to draw a full feather shape each time.

Most of the designs in the Pattern section, or those available as stencils, are drawn with overlapping feathers. If you want to use one of these designs, it can be easily adapted for machine quilting by removing every other feather, as in the Star and Feather border shown below.

Continuous-Line Feathered Wreath

Star and Feather border of JOYFUL HEARTS, machine quilted by the author.

Continuous-Line Running Border

Machine threads cannot travel between the layers of a quilt, from one feather to another, as in hand quilting. However, traditional overlapping feather designs can be quilted in a continuous line by stitching over small areas a second time to move to the next area to be quilted. The re-stitched portion of the design should follow the first line of stitching as closely as possible so it is not distracting.

1. A continuous line of quilting is re-stitched along the center line and across the full part of every other feather plume. Note that dark thread was used for photography purposes. The re-stitched line would be less visible with a light or matching color thread.

2. A continuous line of quilting, every other feather omitted.

3. A pattern of individual feathers, drawn with closer placement than in the previous photo.

4. Overlapping feathers quilted in pairs and tied off at the outside edge, so that the only traveling is done along the center circle. This technique requires several starts and stops, but produces a very clean look with almost no re-stitching.

It is possible, with some thought, to design other patterns that appear much more complex, but can be quilted in a continuous line with only minor re-stitching.

A continuous-line quilting pattern in MEADOW BLOSSOM, designed and machine quilted by the author.

Anita Shackelford: *Infinite Feathers*

Innovative Designs

Some quilts beg for non-traditional quilting motifs, and a few people are naturally inclined to design in this style. Allow yourself some time to play with the Infinite Feathers template. Try something unexpected. Throughout the book, there are suggestions for creative motifs within each style. The following are a few more ideas for drawing unusual or innovative designs.

Use the long, curved #9 feather for pinwheel or rosette designs with a lot of movement.

Turn the feathers around with the pointed tip to the outside for another pinwheel variation.

Use the large, straight #11 feather and a small center circle for a variation of the classic feathered wreath.

Draw a plume in which the feathers curl toward, instead of away from, the spine.

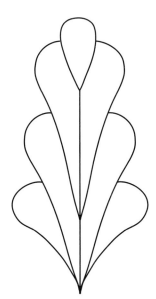

Combine different sizes of feathers in the same motif for an exciting look.

Combine large and small feathers in a double-feathered wreath.

Begin with a paisley or another interesting shape as an outline and fill it with feathers.

Alternate large and small feathers along a spine for a running border, or along the sides of a plume.

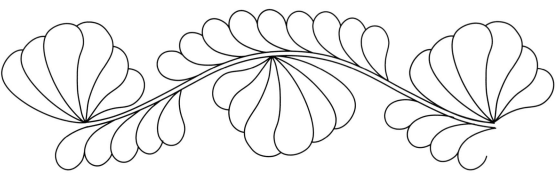

Add other motifs, such as thorns, leaves, flowers, shells, or stars, to a feathered border design.

Anita Shackelford: *Infinite Feathers*

An unusual, asymmetrical arrangement of feathers, repeated four times, makes an interesting block design.

Four feathers from the block can be repeated in line for a companion border.

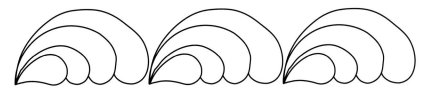

Create a border with a combination of feathers and leaves. Inspired by Gwen Marston's free design style, Sharon Finton, Oakland, Michigan, quilted random groupings of feathers and leaves in the border of her FEATHERED ROSE GARDEN.

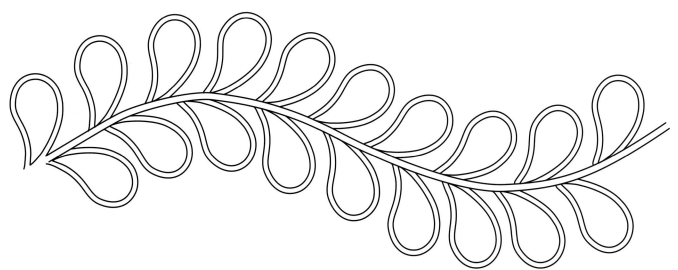

When a design contains isolated feathers, consider quilting a double line around each feather.

Other Creative Feather Motifs

Many other interesting motifs can be created by combining feather shapes. Some of these designs may be appliquéd, as well as quilted. The following are a few ideas for creative combinations.

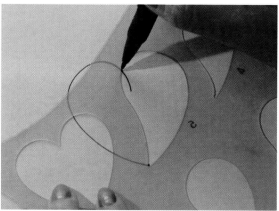

Heart

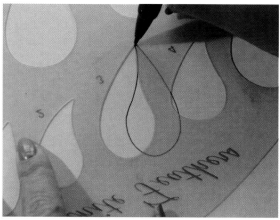

Heart

Heart

A variety of heart shapes can be drawn by combining one feather and its reverse shape.

Draw the curved side of any feather shape.

Flip the template and position the same shape so the point touches the previously drawn point.

Spread the rounded end as far as desired and draw the other half of the heart.

Leaf

Graceful leaves can be drawn in a variety of sizes by combining a feather and its reverse shape.

Draw any complete feather shape.

Flip the template and position the same shape so the point touches the previously drawn point.

Spread the rounded end of the template as far as desired and draw the other half of the leaf.

Leaf

Tulip

Draw any feather shape, with the pointed end up.

Flip the template and position the same shape so the rounded ends overlap partially and the tips point to the outside. Repeat the feather shape to draw the other side of the flower.

With the pointed base of the heart template, add the center petal.

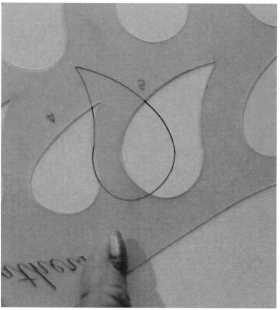

Tulip

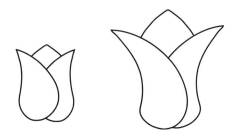

Rosebud

A variety of rosebuds can be drawn by combining two different feather templates.

Draw any feather shape, with the pointed end up.

Flip the template and position the same shape so the rounded ends overlap partially and the pointed ends curve toward the center. Repeat the feather shape to draw the other side of the flower.

Choose a rounded feather plume that fills the space between the points, and trace it to add the flower bud.

Rosebud

Be Creative!

- A few of the sizes on the template work well in combination, such as #3 and #5, #7 and #9.

- Repeat the previous steps to draw a second, inner layer of petals before adding the center. Add a different shape to the flower center with the pointed base of the heart template.*

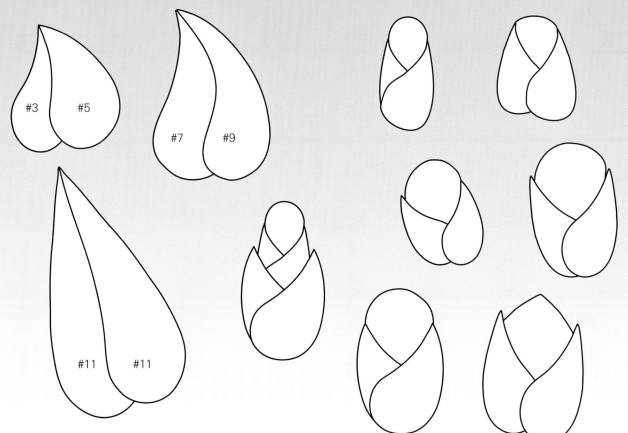

* See pages 145 and 146 for the full-size patterns.

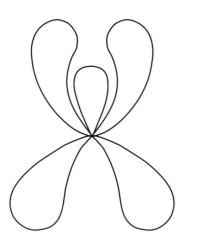

Iris

An iris is created with a combination of straight and curved feathers in a symmetrical arrangement.

Draw the #1 feather for the center of the iris.

Add a petal that curls up around the center. The deeply curved #9 feather is a good choice. Add a bottom petal, positioned to curl down.

Fold the paper in half and copy the petals to the other side.

Wildflower

Draw one feather for a center shape.

Draw one or two feathers on each side to make a cluster of top petals.

Add a feather on each side, positioned to curl down for the base of the flower.

Wildflower and leaves in MEADOW BLOSSOM, made by the author.

Pine Tree

The long #11 feather, repeated in pairs, can be overlapped to draw a tree.

Draw a vertical center guide line. Begin at the top with the tip of the feathers touching the center line, and add as many branches as desired.

Finish the design by drawing a short trunk.

Shell

Draw a center feather. Add several feathers, in progressively smaller sizes, to one side.

Flip the template and add feathers to the other side to make a symmetrical or asymmetrical shape.

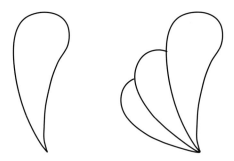

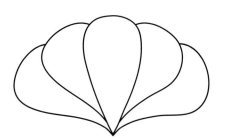

Butterflies

Draw a body and antennae in the size and position desired.

Draw two feathers on the top and two on the bottom for a full view of the butterfly. Two top feathers and a smaller bottom feather, overlapping slightly, create a side view.

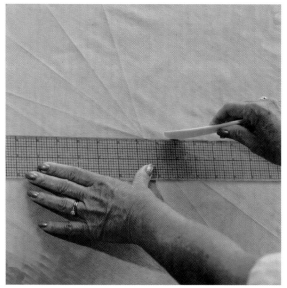

Draw placement lines with a Hera marker.

Direct Drawing

One of the quickest ways to add feather designs to a quilt is to draw them directly onto the quilt top. If you are comfortable with the design process, simply follow the steps for drawing any feather design on the quilt. A Hera marker is a good choice for putting placement lines on the fabric for this direct approach. Drawing directly on the quilt top is also appealing to those who enjoy a more casual or free-form style of design.

If you are working from a paper pattern that you have drawn or taken from the pattern section, the design needs to be transferred to the quilt top. Because patterns might be damaged when the design is transferred to the quilt top, always make a copy of the pattern for working use, and keep the original in a file for the future. Make a dark, accurate copy of the full design. It is helpful if the design includes a center mark and other positioning lines, so the motif can be positioned correctly within the design space.

Light Box

A light box works well for tracing designs onto light-color fabrics.

Copy the design, making sure the lines are dark enough to see through a layer of fabric.

Before the quilt top is assembled, you can work with one block at a time. Tape the pattern to the light box and tape the block over the pattern for easy tracing. If the quilt top is already assembled, tape the pattern to the light box and secure the quilt top by pinning the fabric to the paper pattern. Make sure the pattern is centered in the design space.

With a fabric marker, trace the design onto the quilt top.

Freezer paper eliminates the need to tape or pin the fabric in place. The freezer paper can be ironed to the fabric to keep it from shifting as the design is traced. Because the pattern is reversed, or drawn wrong side up, use this idea for symmetrical designs, or make a reverse copy of an asymmetrical design.

Use a light box to trace designs.

With a dark, permanent marker, trace the design onto the dull side of the freezer paper. Iron the freezer paper to the wrong side of the quilt block or top, making sure the pattern is centered in the design space. Turn the piece right side up and place it over the light box. With a fabric marker, trace the design onto the quilt top.

Transfer Paper

Transfer paper can be used to transfer designs onto any fabric, and is especially helpful with fabrics too dark to trace through. Transfer papers come in a variety of colors for use on light and dark fabrics. Test the marks first for ease of removal.

Make a copy of the design.

On a hard surface, place in layers, the quilt top or block right side up, the transfer paper with the transfer side down, and the quilting design right side up. Make sure the pattern is centered in the design space. It is helpful to tape or pin the layers together before marking.

Use a knitting needle, mechanical pencil (with the lead retracted), or other pointed tool to trace over the design and transfer it to the fabric.

Use transfer paper to trace designs.

Transfer Mesh

A design can be copied onto a sheet of thin plastic mesh and drawn over again to transfer the design onto the fabric.

Make a copy of the design.

Place the transfer mesh over the paper design and copy the design onto the plastic with a pencil. If necessary, mark corners or placement lines on the mesh.

Layer the plastic mesh over the quilt top or block and retrace the design. When the pencil traces over the holes in the plastic mesh, a pattern of dotted lines will be transferred to the fabric.

Retrace design through the mesh.

Antique cardboard templates.

Variety of template materials.

Make stencils from your designs.

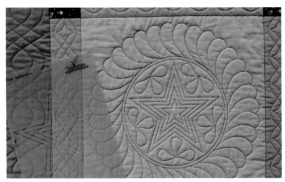

Commercial stencil.

Templates

There are times when it may be simpler to mark a quilting design by tracing around a template rather than copying a line drawing. In the past, metal or cardboard templates were often used to mark quilting designs. Today, plastic, freezer paper, or adhesive paper can be used to make templates. While cardboard or plastic makes more permanent templates, adhesive papers offer the advantage of staying in place while traced. I enjoy working with templates for filler motifs in background areas, especially when I can allow more freedom in the placement of the design.

Another template I use occasionally is a window template. This is particularly helpful when feathers are to be quilted within an appliqué shape. Creating a template of the entire shape, along with the window cut outs, ensures accurate placement of the quilting design each time it is drawn.

Iron the freezer paper to the fabric to trace the pattern.

Window template.

Stencils

One of the most common ways to mark quilting designs is with stencils which have channels cut through a thin sheet of plastic. If you are interested in making stencils from your own quilting designs, ask your local quilt shop or check a mail order source for template plastic and double-blade knives, or stencil burning tools. For excellent instructions on making stencils, refer to the Bibliography, page 159. Some commercial stencils manufacturers will cut designs for individual quiltmakers who request this service.

Anita Shackelford: *Infinite Feathers*

Tear–Away Paper

For machine quilting, a paper pattern can be placed directly on the quilt, eliminating the step of marking the fabric. Copy the design onto paper that will tear away easily. If the same design is to be repeated many times, copies can be made quickly by stacking several papers and stitching through them with an unthreaded needle. The needle holes create designs on all of the papers at once. Pin a single paper in place on the layered quilt and machine quilt along the lines, through the paper and the layers of the quilt. Tear away the paper when the quilting is finished.

Pin the paper in place on the layered quilt.

Machine quilt along the pattern lines.

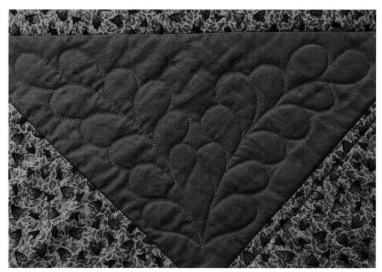

Tear away the paper when finished.

Anita Shackelford: *Infinite Feathers*

Conclusion

Traditionally, feathered designs have been used to fill an entire whole-cloth quilt or to add beautiful detail to alternate blocks and background areas of pieced or appliquéd quilts. But with a little thought, feathers can be used in even more creative ways. When you are ready to mark the quilting designs on your next quilt top, take a little time to see how feathers might be used in some unexpected way.

Soft flowing feathers can make a wonderful design when placed over patchwork, adding texture and visual interest to a pieced quilt. Feathers in Ohio Star block, hand quilted by the author.

Feathers can accent the edges of a swag border or an appliquéd vine as in BIRDS AND BERRIES AND MORE, by Joan Hipsher, Ontario, Ohio. Appliqué pattern by Sue Spargo.

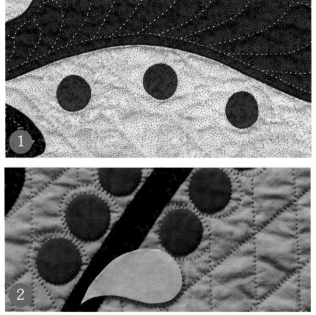

Quilt a single feather to loop around a berry, as in (1) COXCOMB REVISITED, by Sharon Finton, Oakland, Michigan. Or, quilt feathers along a full stem of berries, as in (2) COXCOMB WITH BERRIES, by the author.

Design feather motifs to fit within appliqué shapes. Feather quilting adds beautiful texture and detail to both the small flowers and the large leaves of the COXCOMB ALBUM QUILT, made by the author.

Anita Shackelford: *Infinite Feathers*

COXCOMB WITH BERRIES

47½" x 42½", by Anita Shackelford, 2002. A folk-art red and green quilt features a vase of coxcomb flowers, a bird, and long branches of berries. Feather plumes extend from the vase to accent the design and fill the background space. Hand appliquéd and hand quilted.

WELSH HEART

38" x 38", by Anita Shackelford, 2001. The center design of this wall quilt shows how
a heart-shaped wreath can fill a block on-point. Other quilting includes motifs designed
to fill the setting triangles, straight and undulating feather borders, and small feather
wreaths in the corner blocks. Hand quilted on cotton sateen.

Anita Shackelford: *Infinite Feathers*

My Garden

81" x 81", by Jane Holihan, Walworth, New York, 1995. In her signature style, Jane Holihan quilted a variety of beautiful feather designs to flow and fill the background spaces of this contemporary pictorial quilt. The feathers are well integrated into the overall design of the quilt top. Hand appliquéd and hand quilted with trapunto.

BLUE TULIPS ON PINK SKIES

76" x 81", by Sue Nickels, Ann Arbor, Michigan, 2000. A vertical set gave Sue the opportunity to fill plain strips with a diamond grid and small feathered wreaths in the style of North Country quilts. A feather curl fills the border beautifully and takes a unique turn around the corner. Machine appliquéd and machine quilted.

Anita Shackelford: *Infinite Feathers*

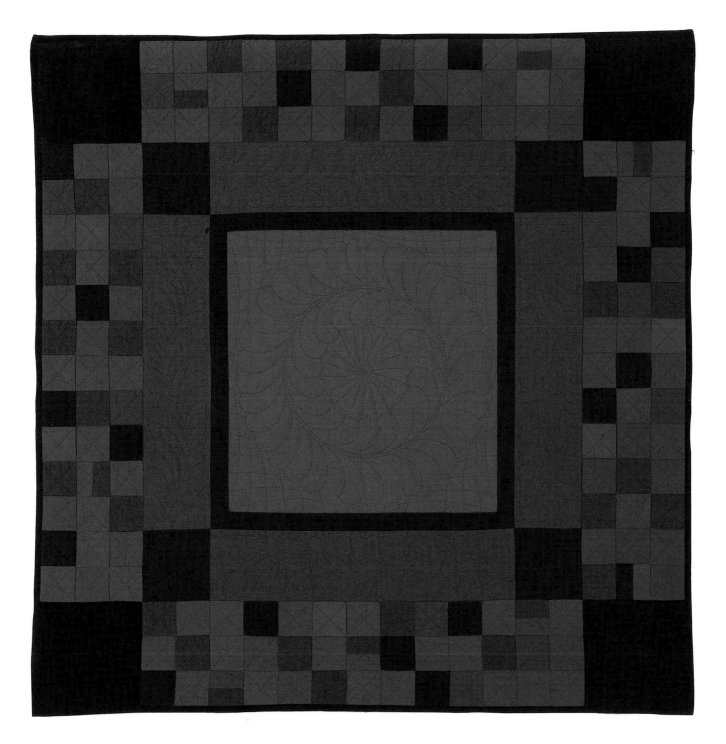

Amish Feathers

38" x 38", by Anita Shackelford, 2001. An Amish-style wall quilt, machine pieced of Cherrywood hand-dyed fabrics, creates the perfect background for fine hand quilting. A large double feather wreath fills the center block. The inner border is filled with an undulating feather design, which flows around the corner. Small feather wreaths fill the outer corner blocks. Machine pieced and hand quilted.

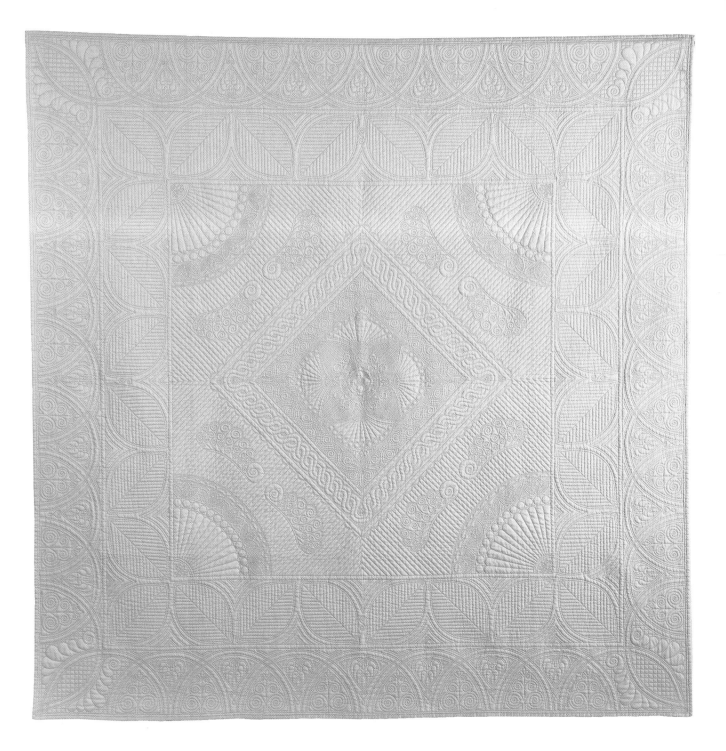

SILVER SPLENDOR

80" x 80", by Andrea Perejda, Arroyo Grande, California, 2000. Andi used a variety of Welsh-style motifs to design this elegant whole-cloth quilt. Feather motifs can be seen within the cathedral arches and in the corner designs, as well as in the gull wings near the center. Hand quilted on cotton sateen. Scallop circle pattern by Dorothy Osler, *Quilting Design Sourcebook*, That Patchwork Place, 1996.

Anita Shackelford: *Infinite Feathers*

Op Amish

83" x 83", Andrea Perejda, Arroyo Grande, California, 1996. Three concentric double feather wreaths create a large medallion center for this Amish-style quilt. A curl border continues the theme and frames the piece beautifully. Hand quilted. Photograph by Sharon Risedorph. Some of the quilting patterns are by Virginia Robertson, *Osage Mountain Quilt Factory Book of Design,* Robertson Enterprises, 1992.

OCTOBER MORNING

82" x 82", by Diane Gaudynski, Pewaukee, Wisconsin, 2000. Well-known for her free-hand machine quilting and beautiful feather designs, Diane has included plumes, feathered hearts, designs which fill triangular spaces, and a border motif which runs from the corner in this spectacular quilt. Machine quilted with trapunto. Rabbit quilting motif by Jeana Kimball, *Fairmeadow*, Foxglove Cottage, 1993.

Anita Shackelford: *Infinite Feathers*

KEEPING STARS IN THE BUTTON BOX

89" x 89", by Ardeth Sveadas, Sparta, Michigan, 1999. Feathers have been added along the edges of several cartouche patterns, designed by Ardie to fit the open spaces in her star sampler medallion quilt. Hand quilted with trapunto.

JAMIE'S JUBILEE

78" x 92", by Barbara Perrin, Grand Rapids, Michigan, 2000. Barbara chose double feathered wreaths and small plumes to fill the open space behind the appliqué in JAMIE'S JUBILEE, which she made for her son's college graduation. She designed the running feather border to repeat in a curl pattern and to flow around the corners perfectly. Hand appliquéd, machine quilted with trapunto.

Anita Shackelford: *Infinite Feathers*

DOUBLE IRISH CHAIN

80" x 100", by Rhoda E. Smith, Benton, New York, 1853. A simple patchwork pattern is made elegant by the addition of feathered wreaths, hearts, pineapples, and lyre shapes quilted in the background areas. Hand quilted with trapunto. Photograph courtesy of the International Quilt Study Center, James Collection, University of Nebraska-Lincoln. 1997.007.0126

Patterns

Over 100 designs, drawn with the Infinite Feathers template, are presented in this section. Many have been enlarged or reduced to fit standard block sizes, or to fit the page. Feel free to copy these designs for your own use. Enlarge or reduce them as needed for your quilt, or use these drawings as inspiration for designs of your own.

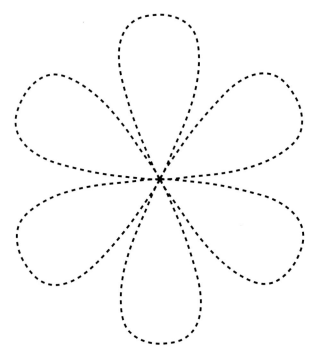

Anita Shackelford: *Infinite Feathers*

Anita Shackelford: *Infinite Feathers*

Anita Shackelford: *Infinite Feathers*

Anita Shackelford: *Infinite Feathers*

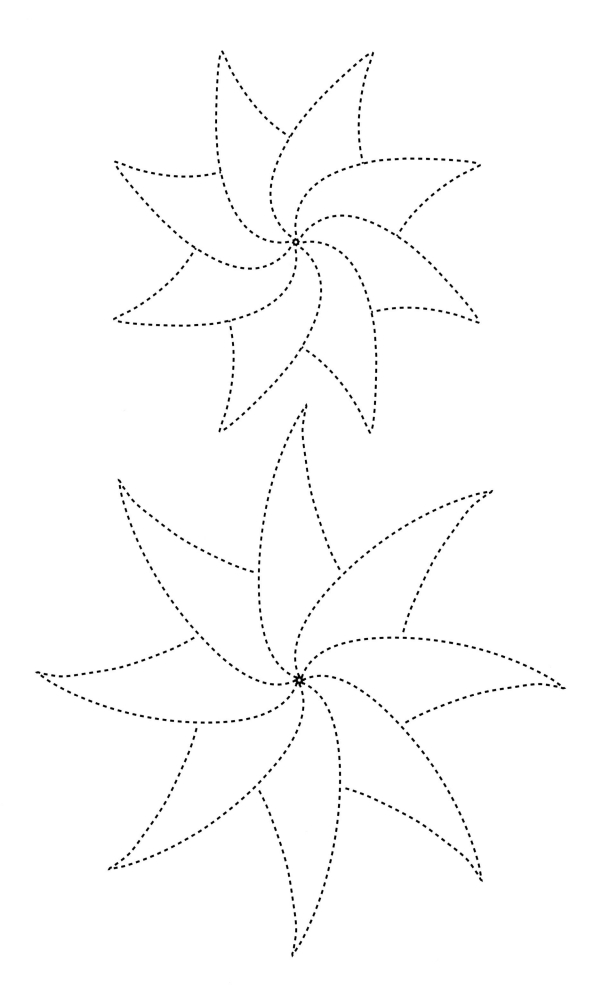

Anita Shackelford: *Infinite Feathers*

Anita Shackelford: *Infinite Feathers*

Anita Shackelford: *Infinite Feathers*

Anita Shackelford: *Infinite Feathers*

Anita Shackelford: *Infinite Feathers*

Anita Shackelford: *Infinite Feathers*

Anita Shackelford: *Infinite Feathers*

Anita Shackelford: *Infinite Feathers*

Anita Shackelford: *Infinite Feathers*

Anita Shackelford: *Infinite Feathers*

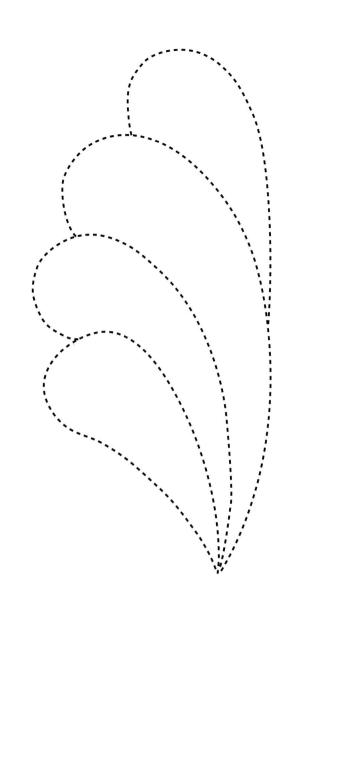
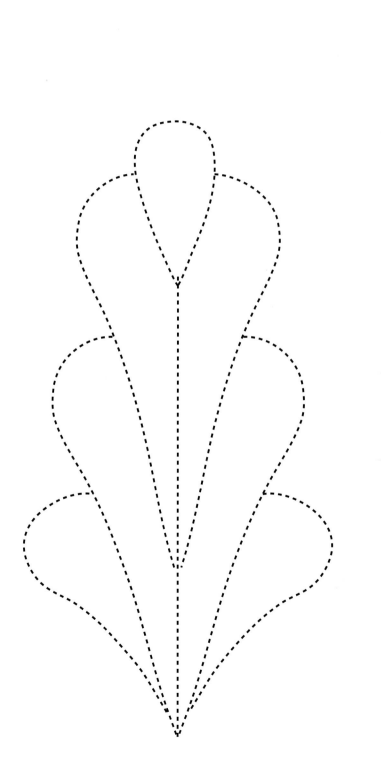

Anita Shackelford: *Infinite Feathers*

Anita Shackelford: *Infinite Feathers*

Anita Shackelford: *Infinite Feathers*

Anita Shackelford: *Infinite Feathers*

Anita Shackelford: *Infinite Feathers*

Anita Shackelford: *Infinite Feathers*

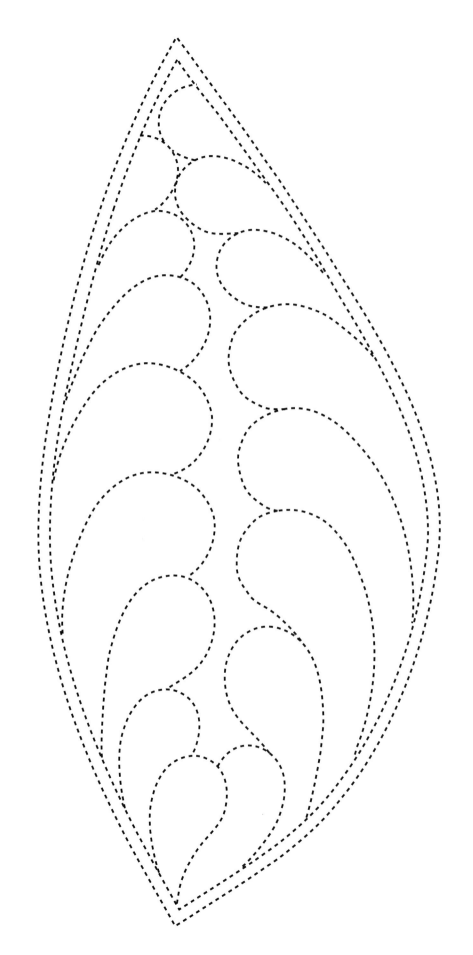

Anita Shackelford: *Infinite Feathers*

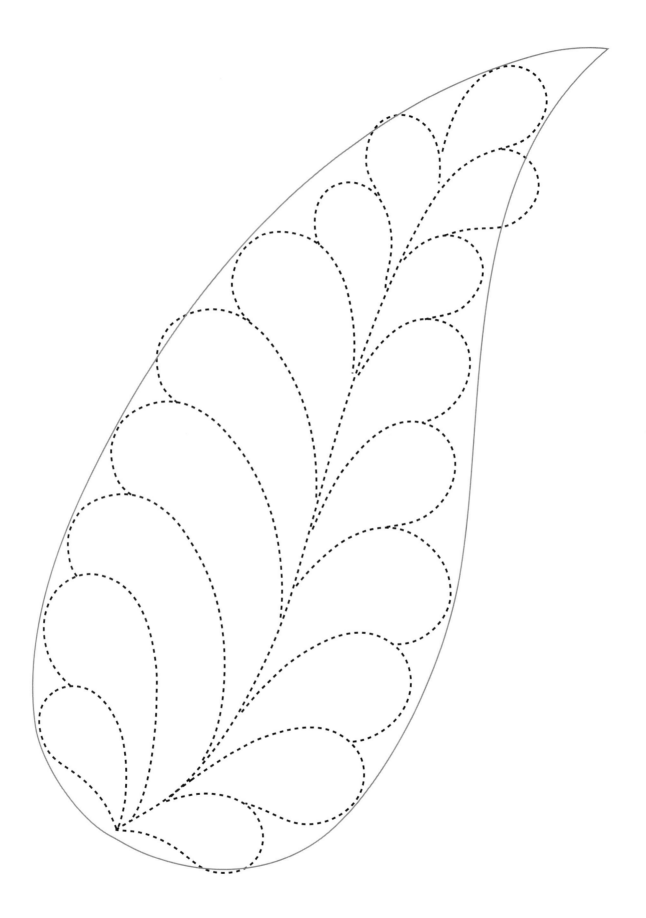

Anita Shackelford: *Infinite Feathers*

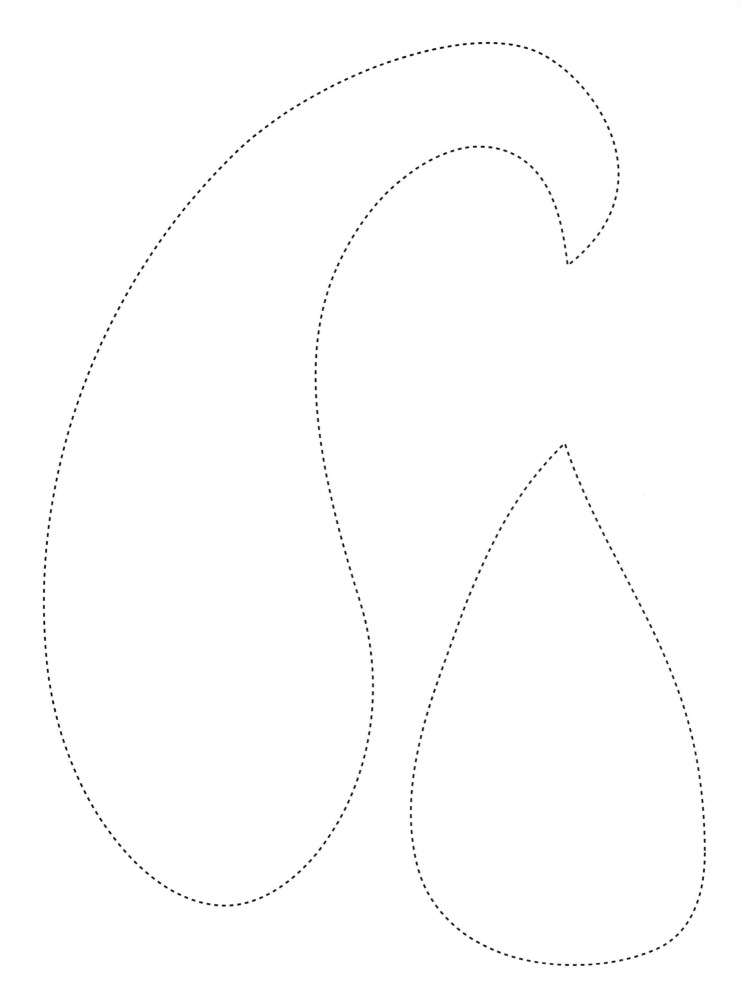

Anita Shackelford: *Infinite Feathers*

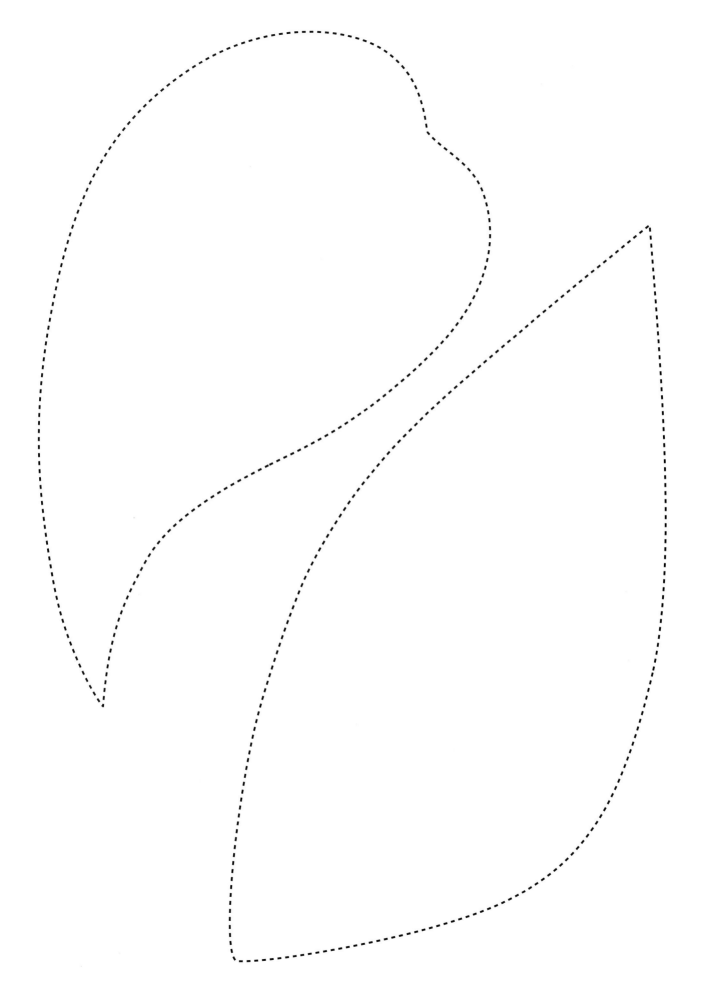

Anita Shackelford: *Infinite Feathers*

Anita Shackelford: *Infinite Feathers*

Anita Shackelford: *Infinite Feathers*

Anita Shackelford: *Infinite Feathers*

Anita Shackelford: *Infinite Feathers*

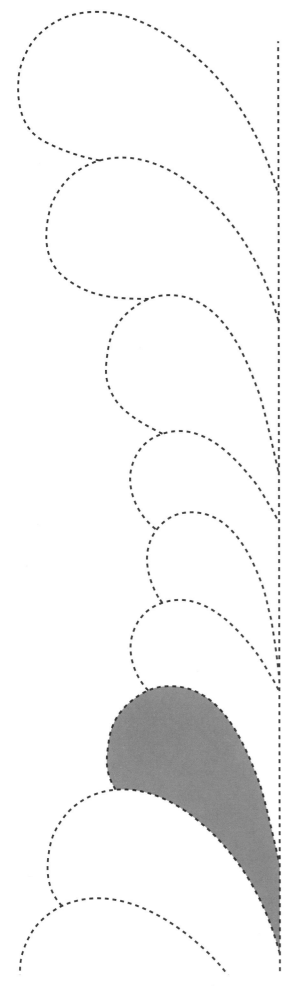
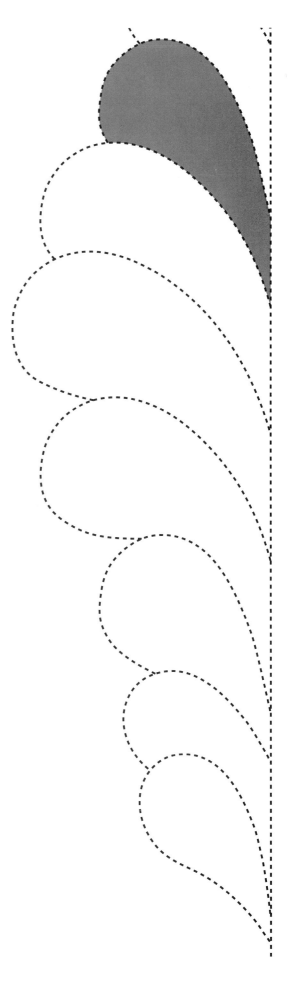

Anita Shackelford: *Infinite Feathers*

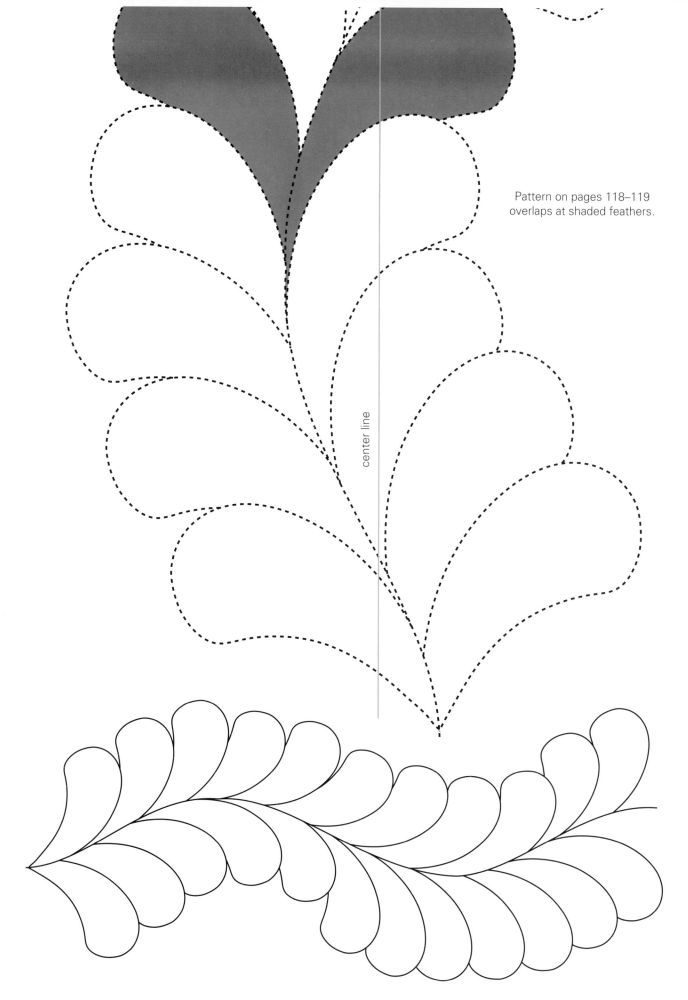

Pattern on pages 118–119
overlaps at shaded feathers.

center line

Anita Shackelford: *Infinite Feathers*

center line

Pattern on pages 118–119
overlaps at shaded feathers.

Anita Shackelford: *Infinite Feathers*

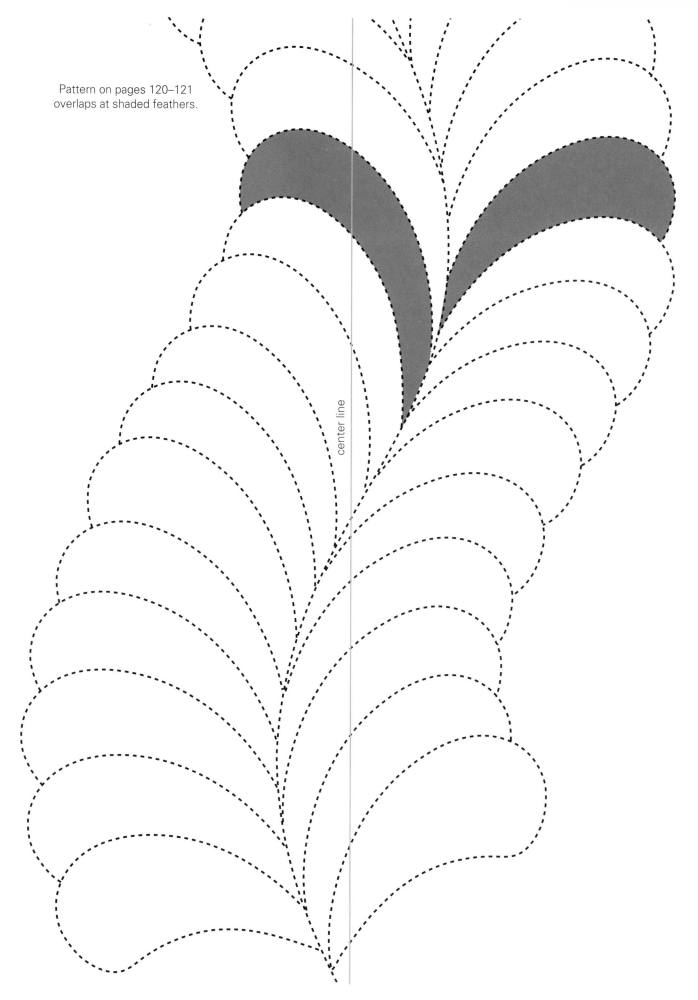

Pattern on pages 120–121
overlaps at shaded feathers.

center line

Anita Shackelford: *Infinite Feathers*

Pattern on pages 120–121 overlaps at shaded feathers.

center line

Anita Shackelford: *Infinite Feathers*

Pattern on pages 122–124
overlaps at shaded feathers.

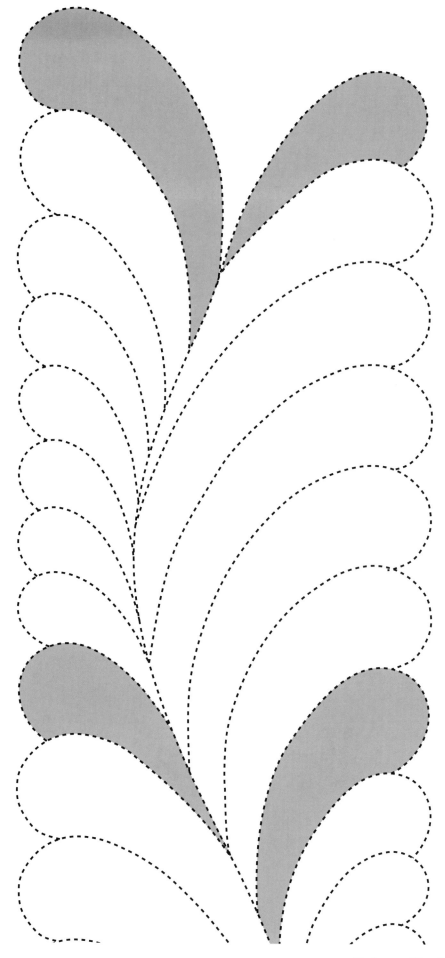

Pattern on pages 122–124
overlaps at shaded feathers.

Pattern on pages 122–124 overlaps at shaded feathers.

Anita Shackelford: *Infinite Feathers*

Pattern on pages 125–126 overlaps at shaded feathers.

center line

Anita Shackelford: *Infinite Feathers*

Pattern on pages 125–126 overlaps at shaded feathers.

center line

Anita Shackelford: *Infinite Feathers*

Pattern on pages 127–129
overlaps at shaded feathers.

border
repeat A

A

center line

border
repeat B

B

B

B

B

A

A

B

B

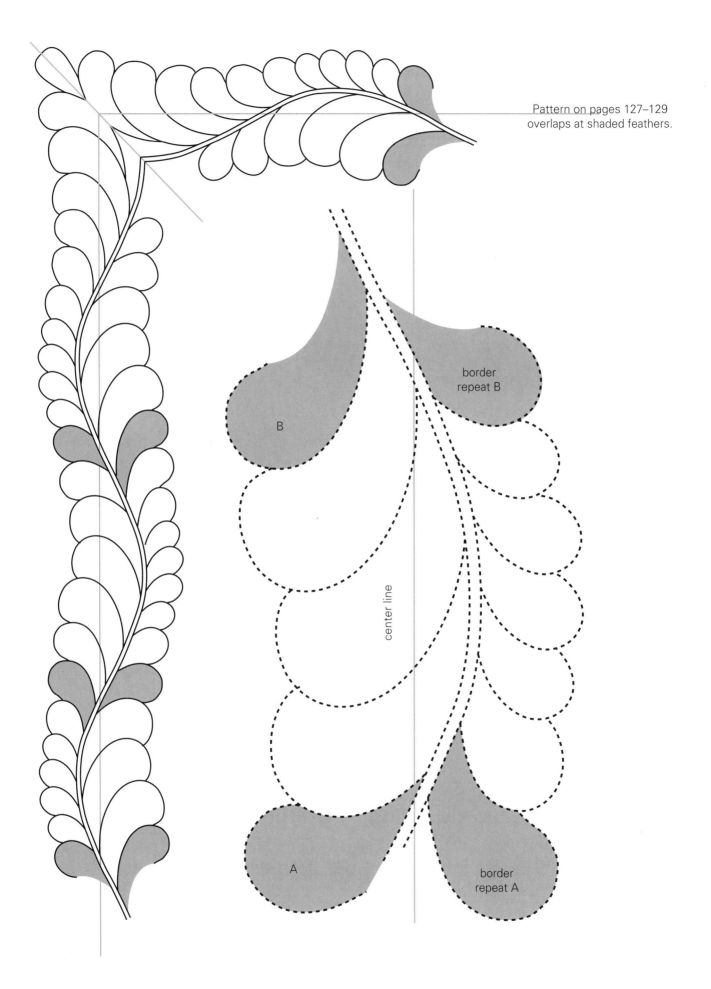

Pattern on pages 127–129
overlaps at shaded feathers.

border
repeat B

B

center line

A

border
repeat A

Anita Shackelford: *Infinite Feathers*

Pattern on pages 127–129
overlaps at shaded feathers.

B

miter line

center line

Pattern on pages 130–131
overlaps at shaded feathers.

center line

Anita Shackelford: *Infinite Feathers*

center line

Pattern on pages 130–131 overlaps at shaded feathers.

Anita Shackelford: *Infinite Feathers*

center line

Anita Shackelford: *Infinite Feathers*

center line

Anita Shackelford: *Infinite Feathers*

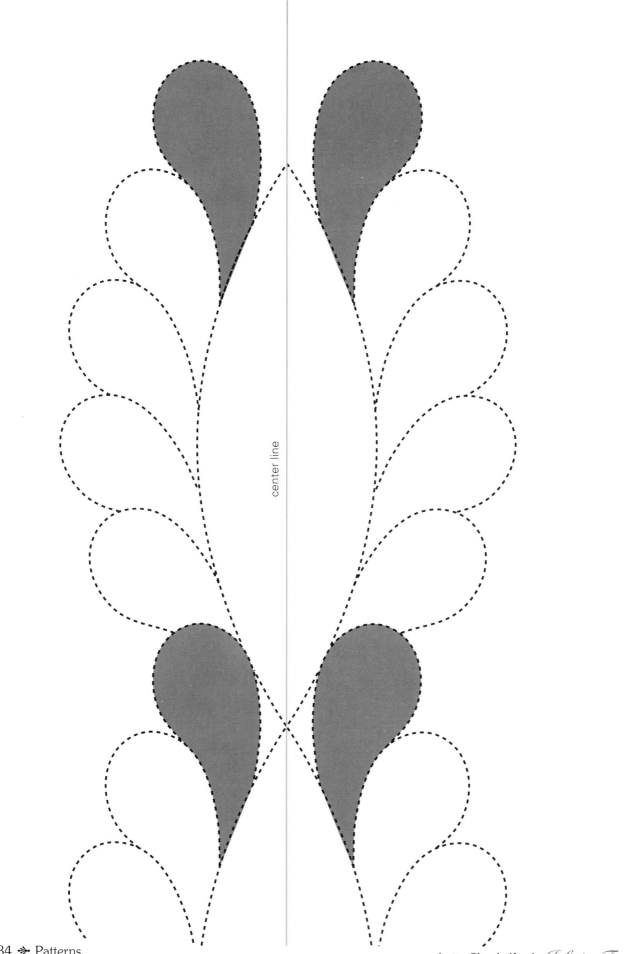

center line

Anita Shackelford: *Infinite Feathers*

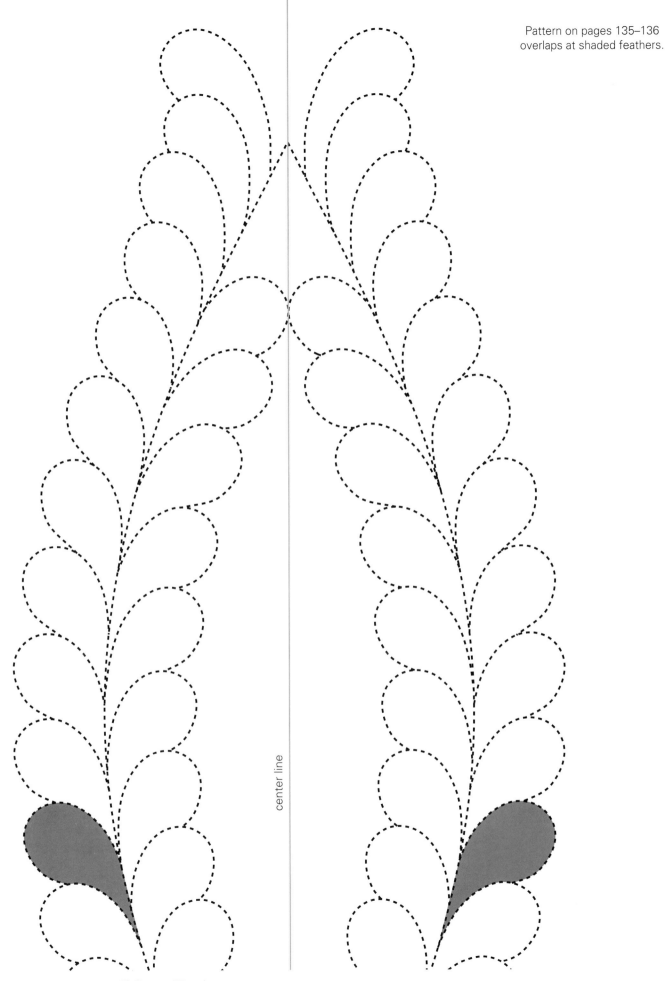

center line

Anita Shackelford: *Infinite Feathers*

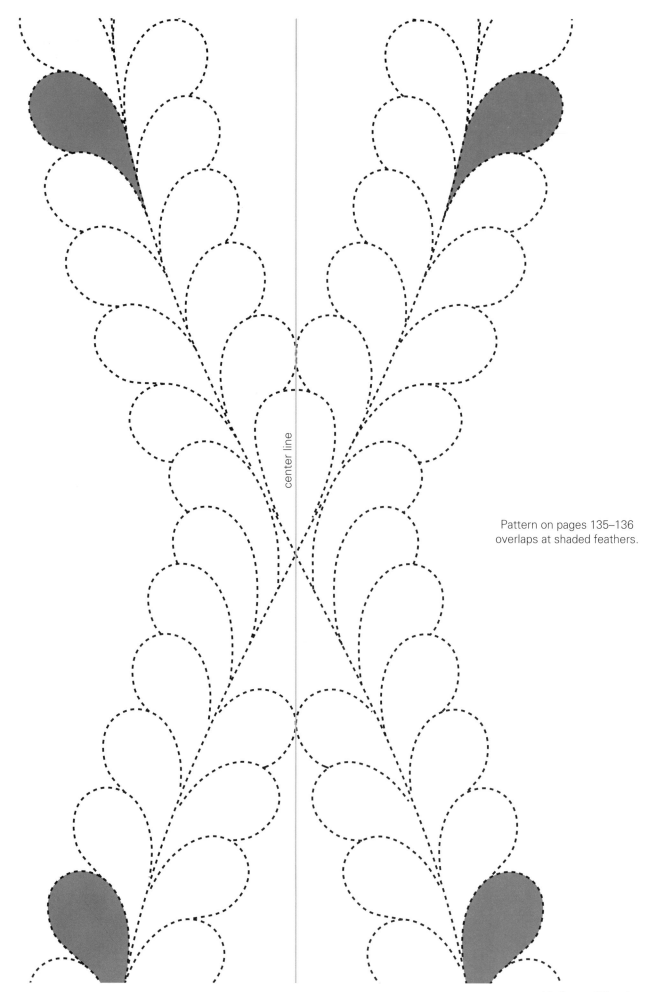

center line

Pattern on pages 135–136
overlaps at shaded feathers.

Anita Shackelford: *Infinite Feathers*

Pattern on pages 137–138
overlaps at shaded feathers.

center line

Anita Shackelford: *Infinite Feathers*

center line

miter line

Pattern on pages 137–138
overlaps at shaded feathers.

Anita Shackelford: *Infinite Feathers*

Anita Shackelford: *Infinite Feathers*

Anita Shackelford: *Infinite Feathers*

Anita Shackelford: *Infinite Feathers*

Anita Shackelford: *Infinite Feathers*

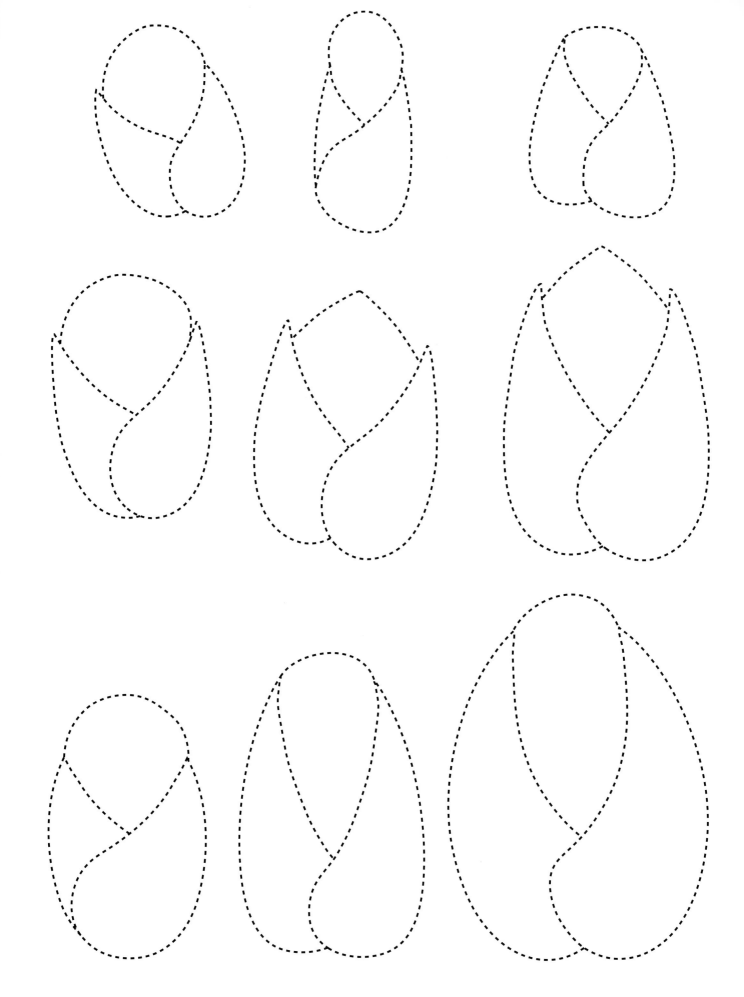

Anita Shackelford: *Infinite Feathers*

center line

Anita Shackelford: *Infinite Feathers*

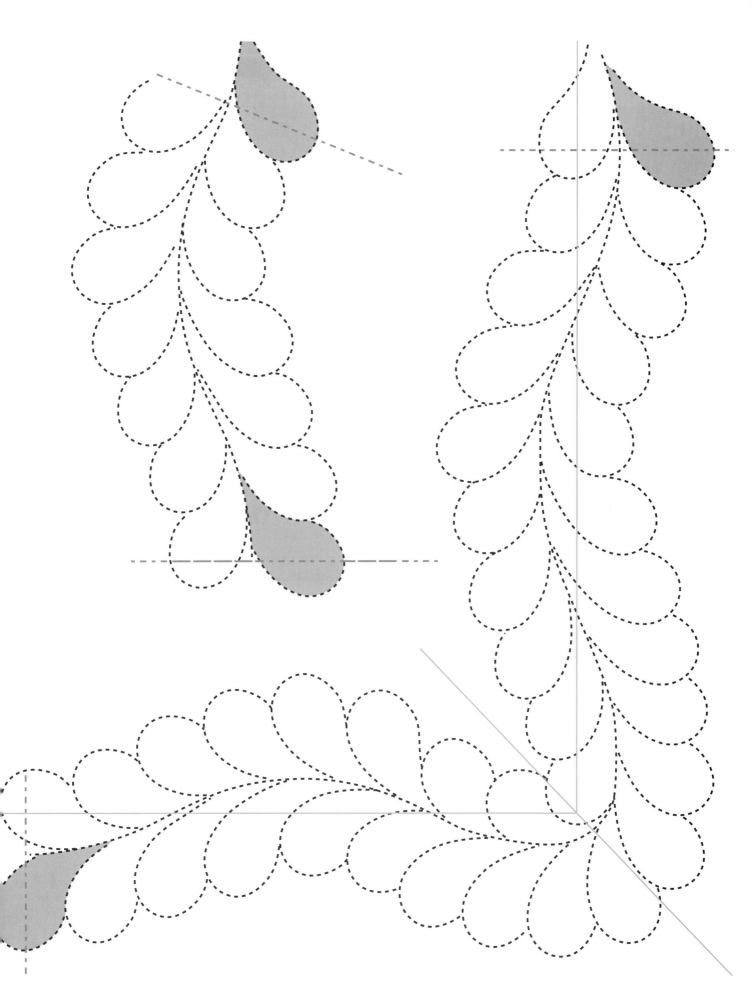

Pattern on pages 150–151
overlaps at shaded feathers.

Anita Shackelford: *Infinite Feathers*

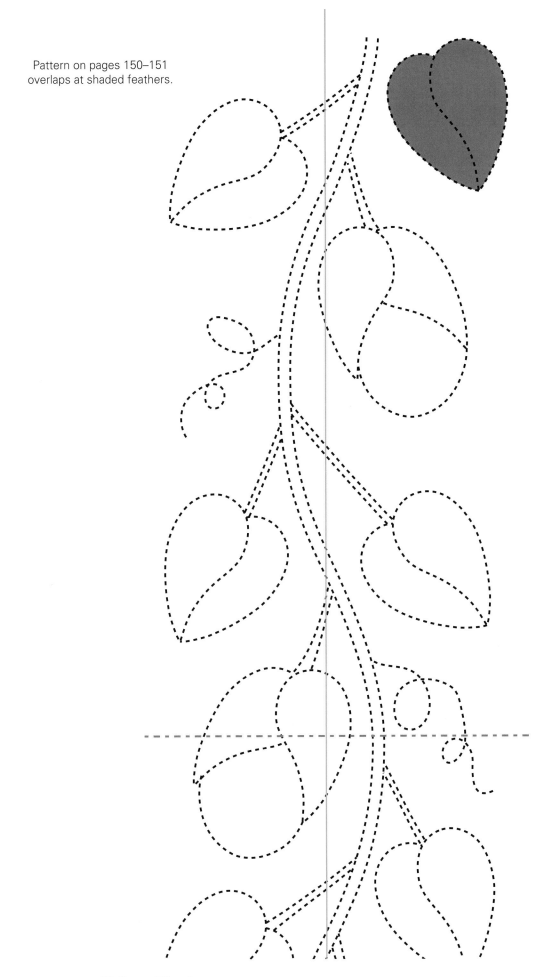

Pattern on pages 150–151
overlaps at shaded feathers.

Anita Shackelford: *Infinite Feathers*

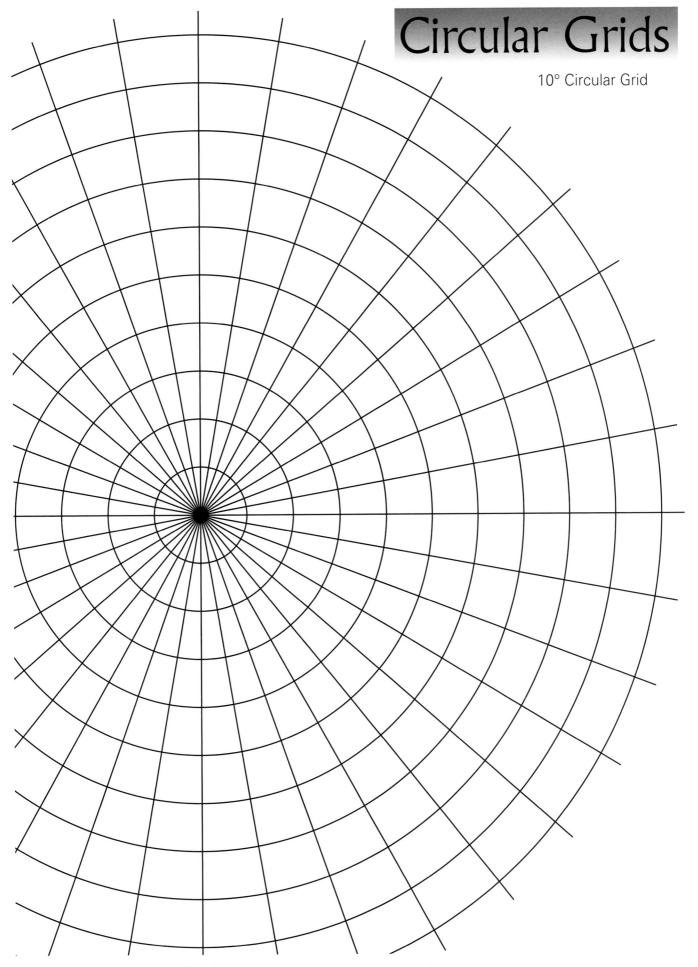

Anita Shackelford: *Infinite Feathers*

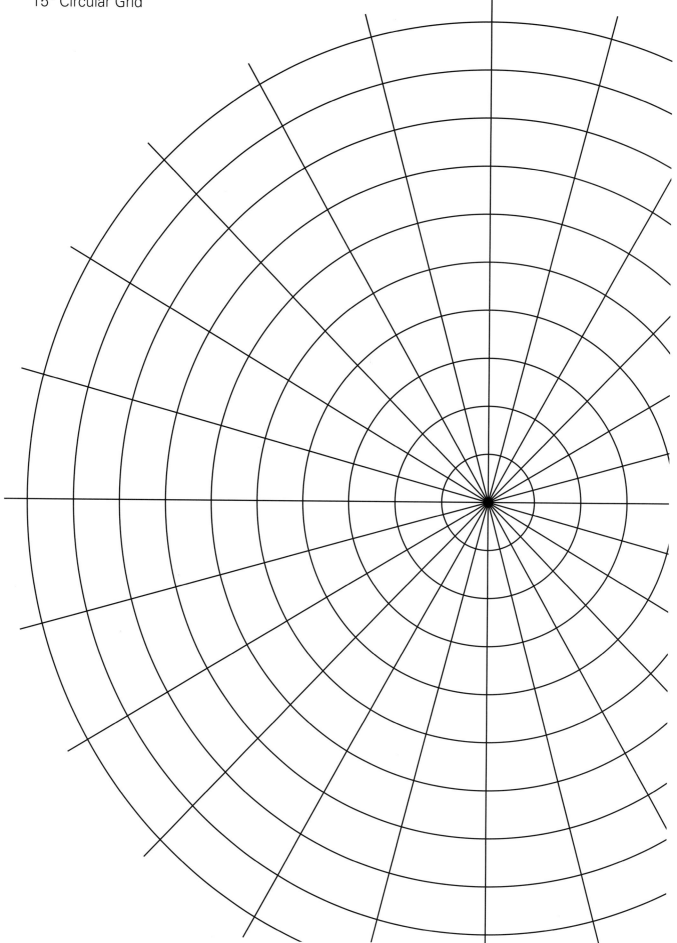

Anita Shackelford: *Infinite Feathers*

Anita Shackelford: *Infinite Feathers*

Anita Shackelford: *Infinite Feathers*

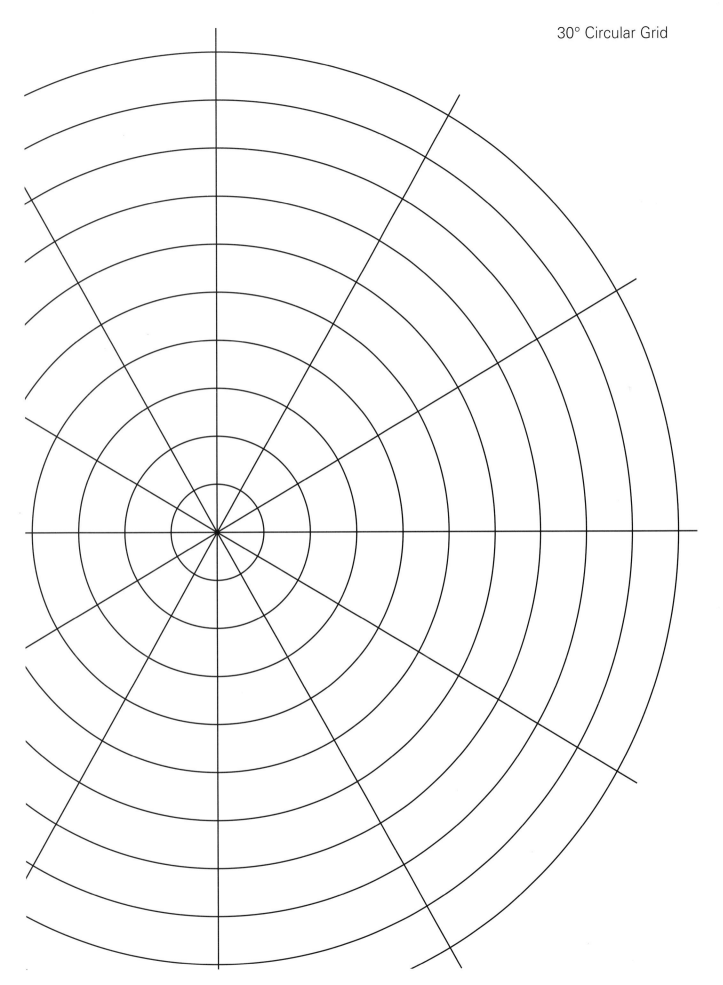

Anita Shackelford: *Infinite Feathers*

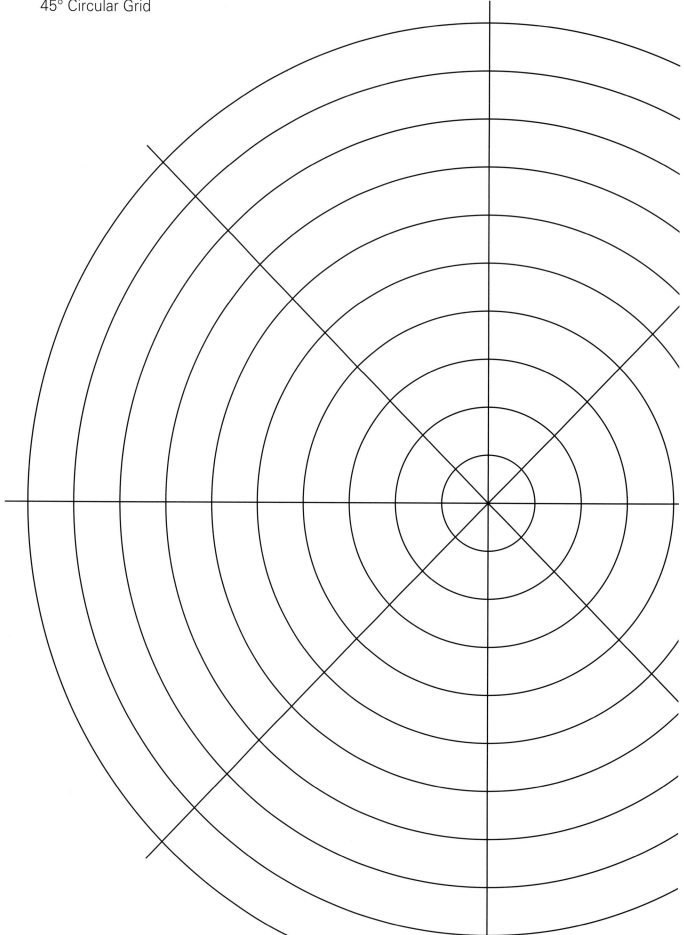

Anita Shackelford: *Infinite Feathers*

Bibliography

Bishop, Robert and Elizabeth Safanda. *A Gallery of Amish Quilts*. New York: E.P. Dutton, Inc., 1976.

Browning, Bonnie K. *Borders & Finishing Touches*. Paducah, KY: American Quilter's Society, 1998.

Cory, Pepper. *Mastering Quilt Marking*. Lafayette, CA: C&T Publishing, 1999.

Hargrave, Harriet. *Heirloom Machine Quilting*. Lafayette, CA: C&T Publishing, 1990.

Marston, Gwen and Jo Cunningham. *Quilting with Style*. Paducah, KY: American Quilter's Society, 1993.

Miller, Phyllis D. *Encyclopedia of Designs for Quilting*. Paducah, KY: American Quilter's Society, 1996.

McElroy, Roxanne. *That Perfect Stitch*. Lincolnwood, IL: Quilt Digest Press, 1998.

Morris, Pat. *Ins & Outs: Perfecting the Quilting Stitch*. Paducah, KY: American Quilter's Society, 1990.

Osler, Dorothy. *North Country Quilts: Legend and Living Tradition*. Durham, United Kingdom: The Bowes Museum Barnard Castle, 2000.

Shackelford, Anita. *Anita Shackelford: Surface Textures*. Paducah, KY: American Quilter's Society, 1997.

Wagner, Debra. *Teach Yourself Machine Piecing and Quilting*. Radnor, PA: Chilton Book Company, 1992.

Resources

**Infinite Feathers Design Template,
Basic Shapes Templates, Perfect Spiral, and quilting design stencils**
Thimble Works
PO Box 462, Bucyrus, OH 44820
Website: www.thimbleworks.com

Quilting paper
Golden Threads
2 S. 373 Seneca Dr.
Wheaton, IL 60187
Phone: 888-477-7718
Website: www.goldenthreads.com
E-mail: info@goldenthreads.com

Saral Transfer paper
Saral Paper Corporation
400 E. 55th St., Suite 14C
New York, NY 10022
Phone: 212-223-3322
Website: www.saralpaper.com
E-mail: info@saralpaper.com

Stencils
Quilting Creations International, Inc.
PO Box 512, Zoar, OH 44697
Phone: 330-874-4741
Website: www.quiltingcreations.com
E-mail: info@quiltingcreations.com

Template and stencil material
Stearns Technical Textiles Co.
100 Williams St.
Cincinnati, OH 45215
Website: www.stearnstextiles.com
E-mail:
    mountainmist@stearnstextiles.com
Phone: 513-948-5275
Ordering: 800-345-7150

Transfer paper/mesh transfer canvas
Clover Needlecraft, Inc.
1007 E. Dominguez St., Suite L
Carson, CA 90746-3620
Phone: 310-516-7846
Ordering: 800-233-1703
E-mail: clovercni@earthlink.net

Stick-n-Stitch™ template shapes
Pieces of the Past
300 N. Dean Rd., Suite 5, PMB 124
Auburn, AL 36830
Phone: 877-784-5833
Website: www.piecesofthepast.com
E-mail: products@piecesofthepast.com

OTHER AQS BOOKS

This is only a small selection of the books available from the American Quilter's Society. AQS books are known worldwide for timely topics, clear writing, beautiful color photos, and accurate illustrations and patterns. The following books are available from your local bookseller, quilt shop, or public library.

#6071   us$22.95

#6069   us$24.95

#6006   us$25.95

#6070   us$24.95

#5706   us$18.95

#5234   us$22.95

#5817   us$16.95

#5849   us$21.95

#5894   us$29.95

Look for these books nationally or call 1-800-626-5420